The Intergovernmental Panel on Climate Change (IPCC) performs one of the most important jobs in the world. It surveys climate science research and writes a report about what it all means. This report is informally known as the Climate Bible.

Cited by governments around the world, the Climate Bible is the reason carbon taxes are being introduced, heating bills are rising, and costly new regulations are being enacted. It is why everyone thinks carbon dioxide emissions are dangerous. Put simply: the entire planet is in a tizzy because of a United Nations report.

What most of us don't know is that, rather than being written by a meticulous, upstanding professional in business attire, the Climate Bible is produced by a slapdash, slovenly teenager who has trouble distinguishing right from wrong.

This exposé, by an investigative journalist, is the product of two years of research. Its conclusion: almost nothing we've been told about the IPCC is true.

The Delinquent Teenager

Who Was Mistaken
for the World's
Top Climate Expert

Donna Laframboise

digital editions of this book are published by
Ivy Avenue Press, Toronto, Canada
IvyAvenue.com

see: TinyUrl.com/bad-teen
and Amazon stores in the UK, Germany & France
for Kindle e-books

for the instantly downloadable, 123-page PDF edition
please visit:
TinyUrl.com/ipcc-expose

There are no real experts, only people who understand their own little pieces of the puzzle. The big picture is a mystery...

Danny Hillis, Millennium bug skeptic, Newsweek, *May 1999*

Science is a mosaic of partial and conflicting visions.

Freeman Dyson, The Scientist as Rebel, *2006*

1 - A CLOSER LOOK AT THE WORLD'S LEADING CLIMATE BODY

This book is about a spoiled child. Year after year, this child has been admired, flattered, and praised. There has been no end of self-esteem-building in his life. What there has been little of, though, is honest feedback or constructive criticism.

When we're young, our parents ensure that we confront our mistakes. When our ball shatters a neighbor's window we're required to apologize - and to help pay for a replacement. What happens, though, if a child is insulated from consequences? What if he hears his parents tell the neighbor that because he's special and precious he hasn't done anything *that* wrong by trampling the neighbor's flower bed?

The answer is obvious. A child who is never corrected is unlikely to develop self-discipline. A child whom everyone says is brilliant feels no need to strive for excellence. Nor does he have much hope of developing what, in this tale, is the most important quality of all: sound judgment.

The child at the center of this book was brought into the world by two United Nations bodies - one focused on the weather, the other on the environment. Called the Intergovernmental Panel on Climate Change - IPCC for short - this child arrived more than 20 years ago. [note 1-1]

Notice that the word *intergovernmental* is part of its name. This means that every country that chooses to send delegates to infrequent meetings is a godparent of the IPCC. Any child with over 100 godparents is bound to be spoiled. Even when he torments small animals there will always be those who think he can do no wrong.

Which means that disciplining this child is next to impossible.

Having morphed into an obnoxious adolescent, the IPCC is now everyone's problem. This is because it performs one of the most important jobs in the world. Its purpose is to survey the scientific literature regarding climate change, to decide what it all means, and to write an ongoing series of reports. These reports are informally known as the Climate Bible.

The Climate Bible is cited by governments around the world. It is the reason carbon taxes are being introduced, heating bills are rising, and costly new regulations are being enacted. It is why everyone thinks carbon dioxide emissions are dangerous.

Put simply: the entire planet is in a tizzy because of a UN report. What most of us don't know is that, rather than being written by a meticulous, upstanding professional in business attire, this report was produced by a slapdash, slovenly teenager who has trouble distinguishing right from wrong.

For now, let us consider just one example. In the grown-up world, whenever important decisions and large amounts of money are involved conflict-of-interest mechanisms are firmly in place. Lawyers, accountants, politicians, and many others are subject to these rules as a matter-of-course. People who expect to be trusted by the public adopted them long ago.

Yet even though the IPCC is one of the world's most influential bodies, and even though it evaluates matters in which trillions of dollars are at stake, well into the 21st century it saw no need to even discuss conflict-of-interest. This organization is so arrogant, so used to being fawned over, that its leaders failed to take the most ordinary of precautions.

2 - SHOWERED WITH PRAISE

The IPCC has lounged, for more than two decades, in a large comfy chair atop a pedestal. When the IPCC is mentioned in broadcasts, newspapers, and books it is portrayed as a paragon of scientific truth and authority. Here are some direct quotes from people describing the IPCC:

- phenomenally successful
- a remarkable history of accomplishments
- there is not a parallel on this planet, in any field of endeavour
- its place in the history books is clear
- if the IPCC says something, you had better believe it [note 2-1]

Journalists are among the IPCC's most ardent admirers. They say the Climate Bible is written by thousands of the world's top experts who all agree with its conclusions. They routinely use words such as *gold standard*, *authoritative*, and *pre-eminent* to describe it. Indeed, when discussing the IPCC the media sound more like cheerleaders than hard-nosed reporters:

- the IPCC...has shown us the way (*Time* magazine)

er and verse, it is Holy Writ (Irish
ent)

ientists have been awed by the IPCC's
ate work (*New York Times*)

greatest feat of global scientific cooperation ever
seen...utterly unique and authoritative (UK
Guardian) [note 2-2]

In 2007, the Nobel committee joined the chorus of praise
singers and crowned the IPCC with a Nobel Peace Prize.
During his presentation speech, the Nobel chairman thanked
the IPCC for its "outstanding scientific work" and for all it
has done "for mother earth." According to the Nobel committee, although it was once unclear whether human activities
were causing global warming, "Thanks to the IPCC there is
very little such doubt today."

If you know a bit about history, though, that Nobel
speech may have left you uneasy. This is how it ended: "Action is needed now. Climate changes are already moving beyond human control." [note 2-3]

Let us be sensible for a moment. Planet Earth is 4.5 billion years old. During that time it has endured all sorts of perfectly natural climate transformations. As recently as 20,000
years ago 97% of Canada was covered by ice. [note 2-4] That
ice melted and retreated and the Ice Age ended all on its
own. The Egyptian pharaohs, remember, only came into the
picture 5,000 years ago, while the Romans ruled 2,000 years
ago. To suggest that the climate has ever been within *human
control* is surely a bit silly.

Mark Twain once observed that:

> ...people's beliefs and convictions are in almost every
> case gotten at second-hand, and without examination,
> from authorities who have not themselves examined the
> questions at issue but have taken them at second-hand
> from other non-examiners, whose opinions about them
> were not worth a brass farthing.

If Twain were alive today, he might have sharp words
for all the hype surrounding the IPCC. Twain was talking

about religion and politics when he made the above remarks and, for some people, environmentalism has become a substitute religion. It is their worldview, the lens through which they interpret everything. Moreover, because the IPCC is a child of the United Nations - the stage on which so many of the world's power blocs jostle with one another - whether we like it or not the IPCC is also mixed up with politics.

It has long been fashionable to be green. For half a century we've taught our children that the planet is fragile, that humans treat it carelessly, and that we are on the brink of ecological disaster. Smart individuals armed with plenty of facts and figures argue that the opposite is actually the case. They say the state of the world is steadily improving, that it's becoming cleaner and healthier. But their voices barely register.

The larger point is that because we have been told so frequently that humans are a threat to the planet we are all *predisposed* to believe that our actions might trigger dangerous climate change. Most of us have never seriously questioned this idea. Among us are prime ministers, regulators, and supreme court judges. Among us are educators, community activists, and parents understandably concerned about the world their children will inherit.

This is why the IPCC has received so little scrutiny. This is why no one noticed that conflict-of-interest guidelines were missing. We all made the mistake of believing the IPCC was a gem of an organization simply because it is connected to protecting the environment.

Closer examination reveals that many of the things we've been told about the IPCC are mistaken. For instance, a great deal of noise is made about the allegedly rigorous manner in which its reports get written. The implication is that the IPCC has procedures and that these procedures are followed diligently.

But while the IPCC has taken the time to write down some rules of the road, it has never hired any traffic cops. Since many people exceed the speed limit when police officers are plentiful, what do we suppose happens when they're entirely absent?

In the real world, when undisciplined youngsters slide behind the wheel of a fast car, how many of them can be counted on to behave?

3 – THE TOP SCIENTISTS & BEST EXPERTS?

The people who write IPCC reports are the *crème de la crème*. Everyone says so. Rajendra Pachauri, the person who has been the IPCC's chairman since 2002, tells us this repeatedly. In 2007 he explained to a newspaper how his organization selects individuals to help write the Climate Bible:

> These are people who have been chosen on the basis of their track record, on their record of publications, on the research that they have done...They are people who are at the top of their profession...

Two years later, when testifying before a committee of the US Senate, Pachauri argued that "all rational persons" should be persuaded by the IPCC's conclusions since his organization mobilizes "the best talent available across the world."

Whether he speaks in Austria or Australia, whether he gives an interview or writes articles himself, Pachauri says he "can't think of a better set of qualified people" to write IPCC reports. At various times he has said the IPCC consists of:

- thousands of the best scientists

- the best scientific expertise from around the world
- almost four thousand of the world's best specialists [note 3-1]

Nor is he the only one to make such claims. Robert Watson, who chaired the IPCC for the five years before Pachauri took over, also says the "IPCC engages thousands of the world's best experts." Media outlets have repeated these assertions time and again.

But such claims are bogus. For starters, some of the world's most experienced experts have been left out in the cold. In 2005 an atmospheric science professor from Colorado State University named William Gray told a US Senate Committee:

Despite my 50 years of meteorology experience and my many years of involvement in seasonal hurricane and climate prediction, I have never been asked for input on any of the [IPCC] reports.

The reason he wasn't invited to the party, he says, is because he doesn't think global warming causes more (or stronger) hurricanes. "They know my views and do not wish to have to deal with them."

Six months prior to Gray's testimony, an expert on the other side of the Atlantic was raising his own concerns before a committee of the British House of Lords. Paul Reiter knows little about atmospheric science. What he does know is the field in which he has specialized for more than 40 years - diseases that are spread by mosquitoes. According to him, the people who've been writing about those diseases in the Climate Bible are not experts.

While a large portion of the health chapter in the 1995 edition dealt with malaria, Reiter points out that "not one of the lead authors had ever written a research paper on the subject!" Only those with limited knowledge of this field, he says, could have produced such "amateurish" work.

For example, the Climate Bible said malaria-transmitting mosquitoes usually don't survive in areas where winter temperatures drop below 16°C (60°F). Reiter says that's nonsense. We now associate malaria with tropical locales, but poverty and an absence of health care are important factors. Hawaii, Aruba, and Barbados are all tropical, but malaria isn't a problem there. On the other hand, in the 1800s thousands died of malaria in North America and Europe - even in Siberia. [note 3-2]

It's the same story with sea levels. The former president of a Commission on Sea Level Change, Nils-Axel Mörner, also addressed the House of Lords committee. Mörner, who has 40 years experience in his field, called attention to the disparity between what genuine sea level specialists think and what those who write IPCC reports believe. Those in the second group, he says, lack hands-on expertise. Instead, they attempt to predict the future via mathematical formulas that have been fed into computers (computer modeling).

Mörner told the House of Lords that, between 1999 and 2003, genuine sea level experts held five international meetings to discuss the available real-world evidence. They concluded that sea levels are unlikely to increase by more than 10 cm (4 inches) by the year 2100. Mörner says the claim that sea levels are rising quickly - or that entire island nations are in imminent danger of drowning - are simply not true.

Dr. Gray, the hurricane specialist, resides in America. Dr. Reiter, the malaria expert, works at the Pasteur Institute in Paris. Dr. Mörner is the former head of a geodynamics unit at the University of Stockholm, in Sweden.

Each of them possesses highly specialized knowledge. Each of them is a seasoned professional with long experience in his field. They are, in other words, exactly the kind of people you'd expect to find at the heart of an organization comprised of world-class scientists examining one of the planet's most important questions.

But they are all IPCC outsiders. This suggests the IPCC defines *top scientists* and *best experts* differently than do most of us.

4 – TWENTY-SOMETHING GRADUATE STUDENTS

So if malaria experts aren't writing the section on malaria in the Climate Bible and world-renowned sea level experts aren't writing the section on sea levels, who is writing IPCC reports?

One group consists of graduate students. Typically these are individuals in their twenties. Their experience of the world is neither broad nor deep. If they were merely performing administrative tasks that would be one thing. But the IPCC has long relied on their expert judgment.

Richard Klein, now a Dutch geography professor, is a classic example. In 1992 Klein turned 23, completed a Masters degree, and worked as a Greenpeace campaigner. Two years later, at the tender age of 25, he found himself serving as an IPCC lead author.

(The IPCC has three classes of writers. *Coordinating lead authors* are in charge of an entire chapter and are therefore the most senior in rank. Each chapter usually has two. *Lead authors* are expected to write a significant amount of text. Their numbers vary from a handful to several dozen. *Contributing authors* provide supplemental knowledge. They typically don't participate in the meetings attended by the other two kinds of authors, but are asked to write briefly about a narrow, specific topic. A chapter may have no contributing authors or as many as 20 of them.)

Klein's online biography tells us that, since 1994, he has been a lead author for six IPCC reports. On three of those occasions, beginning in 1997, he served as a coordinating lead author. This means that Klein was promoted to the IPCC's most senior author role at age 28 - six years *prior* to the 2003 completion of his PhD. Neither his youth nor his thin academic credentials prevented the IPCC from regarding him as one of the world's top experts. [note 4-1]

Nor is he an isolated case. Laurens Bouwer is currently employed by an environmental studies institute at the VU University Amsterdam. In 1999-2000, he served as an IPCC lead author before earning his *Masters* in 2001.

How can a young man without even a Masters degree become an IPCC lead author? Good question. Nor is it the only one. Bouwer's expertise is in climate change and water resources. Yet the chapter for which he first served as a lead author was titled *Insurance and Other Financial Services*.

It turns out that, during part of 2000, Bouwer was a trainee at Munich Reinsurance Company. This means the IPCC chose as a lead author someone who a) was a trainee, b) lacked a Masters degree, and c) was still a full decade away from receiving his 2010 PhD.

Who else falls into this category? Step forward Lisa Alexander. As recently as 2008, this woman was a research assistant at Australia's Monash University. After earning her PhD in 2009, she was hired by another Aussie university - which noted in its announcement that she had already "played a key role" in both the 2001 and 2007 editions of the Climate Bible. (She was a contributing author the first time, and a lead author the second.)

The IPCC selected its 2001 authors during 1999. This means its leadership decided that Alexander was a world-class expert 10 years before she, too, had earned her doctorate.

Sari Kovats, currently a lecturer at the London School of Hygiene and Tropical Medicine, is an even more egregious example. She didn't earn her PhD until 2010. Yet back in 1994 - 16 years prior to that event and three years before her first academic paper was published - Kovats was one of only

21 people in the entire world selected to work on the first IPCC chapter that examined how climate change might affect human health. In total, Kovats has been an IPCC lead author twice and a contributing author once - all long before she'd completed her PhD.

One of Kovats' health chapter colleagues was an American named Jonathan Patz. He earned a Masters degree in Public Health in 1992 and had his first academic paper published in late 1995. Yet in 1994 the IPCC judged his credentials so impressive he was appointed one of its lead authors.

Given the involvement of both Kovats and Patz, Paul Reiter's description of the IPCC's 1995 health chapter as *amateurish* starts to make sense. Rather than recruiting real experts like Reiter the IPCC enlisted young, inexperienced, non-experts instead.

It has been doing so since the mid-1990s. Yet in 2011 newspapers still report that the IPCC is a collection of "the world's leading scientists."

5 – THE RIGHT GENDER OR THE RIGHT COUNTRY

In early 2010 the InterAcademy Council, an organization comprised of science bodies from around the world, took an historic step. It established a committee whose purpose was to investigate IPCC policies and procedures. [note 5-1]

The committee posted a questionnaire on its website and invited interested parties to respond. Answers to those questionnaires were eventually made public after the names of the respondents had been removed. Those provided by IPCC insiders can be separated from the ones submitted by concerned citizens because the questionnaire begins by asking what role the respondent has played in the IPCC. [note 5-2]

People with direct experience of this organization were remarkably frank in their feedback. According to them, scientific excellence isn't the only reason individuals are invited to participate in the IPCC.

Remember, this is a UN body. It therefore cares about the same things other UN bodies care about. Things like diversity. Gender balance. Regional representation. The degree to which developing countries are represented compared to developed countries.

The collected answers to the questionnaire total 678 pages. As early as page 16, someone complains that: "some the lead authors...are clearly not qualified to be lead authors." Here are other direct quotes:

- There are far too many politically correct appointments, so that developing country scientists are appointed who have insufficient scientific competence to do anything useful. This is reasonable if it is regarded as a learning experience, but in my chapter ...we had half of the [lead authors] who were not competent. (p. 138)
- The whole process...[is] flawed by an excessive concern for geographical balance. All decisions are political before being scientific. (p. 554)
- half of the authors are there for simply representing different parts of the world. (p. 296)

Lest anyone think that people from less affluent countries were being unjustly stereotyped, the person whose comments appear on page 330 agrees:

The team members from the developing countries (including myself) were made to feel welcome and accepted as part of the team. In reality we were out of our intellectual depth as meaningful contributors to the process.

The questionnaire did not contain the word *gender*. Nevertheless, it is uttered dozens of times in the answers people provided. While some feel the IPCC should not aim for gender balance, others applaud the use of this selection criteria.

Among those with firsthand IPCC experience, therefore, it is an open secret that some people are appointed for reasons that have little to do with world-class scientific expertise. Depending on whose opinion you believe, this is true in either a small minority of cases or with regard to as many as half of the authors. In the view of at least one person, *every* IPCC personnel decision is influenced by concerns unrelated to science.

If the United Nations regards the IPCC as a training ground for scientists from the developing world that's perfectly OK. If it thinks one of the main goals of the IPCC is to raise the profile of female scientists that's OK, too. It is entitled to do whatever it wants with its own organization. But it is dishonest to tell the world you've assembled a group of competitive cyclists when many on your team are actually riding tricycles.

Journalists say we should trust the IPCC's conclusions because its reports have been written by the world's finest scientific minds. But in order for that to be the case the IPCC would need to apply very different criteria when selecting its authors.

It would need an explicit policy that says something along the lines of: *Even though we are a UN body, we are not influenced by UN diversity concerns. We select the world's best experts and only the best experts - regardless of where they come from or what gender they happen to be.*

That is the kind of IPCC I could believe in. But that is not the IPCC we have.

6 - ACTIVISTS

Many environmental organizations employ people whose sole purpose is to raise awareness about global warming. The more effective these people are at convincing the public there's an urgent problem, the more money we're likely to contribute to their cause.

Since activists bring their own agenda to the table, and since agendas and science don't mix, environmentalists need to keep their distance from scientific endeavors. Data cannot be considered scientifically reputable if it has been collected and analyzed by activists. Scientific conclusions - especially those involving judgment calls - cannot be trusted if activists have played a role.

But activists have not kept their distance from the IPCC. Nor has that organization taken steps to safeguard its reputation by maintaining a strict boundary between itself and green groups. This is one of those red flags, an indicator that the IPCC is a spoiled child that feels no need to conduct its affairs in a grown-up, professional manner.

The improper relationship between activists and the IPCC is illustrated by a 2007 Greenpeace publication. The foreword to that document was written by none other than Rajendra Pachauri. At the end of his remarks, beside his photograph, he is identified not as a private individual expressing private opinions but as the chairman of the IPCC.

The following year Pachauri wrote another foreword for another Greenpeace publication. Think about this for a moment. The IPCC's role is similar to that of a trial judge. It examines the scientific evidence and decides whether or not human-produced carbon dioxide is guilty of triggering climate change.

How much faith would you have in the impartiality of a murder trial if the judge was hearing evidence during the day and partying with the prosecution team during the evening?

As has been mentioned above, the fact that Richard Klein worked as a Greenpeace campaigner at age 23 was no impediment to the IPCC appointing him a lead author at age 25. But that's just the beginning.

Bill Hare has been a Greenpeace spokesperson since 1992 and served as its 'chief climate negotiator' in 2007. A Greenpeace blog post describes him as a *legend* in that organization. Yet none of this has prevented him from filling senior IPCC roles.

When the 2007 edition of the Climate Bible was released, we learned that Hare had served as a lead author, that he'd been an expert reviewer for two out of three sections of the report, and that he was one of only 40 people on the "core writing team" for the overall, big-picture summary known as the *Synthesis Report*.

It's worth noting that the IPCC is less-than-candid about Hare's Greenpeace ties. The 2007 Climate Bible lists his affiliation as the Potsdam Institute for Climate Impact Research in Germany. Since Hare is a 'visiting scientist' there the IPCC hasn't lied. Nevertheless, it has committed a sin of omission. His Greenpeace affiliation means he's not just any researcher.

Imagine you're an accident victim on the side of the road. You're told not to worry, that the person who's going to remain with you until the ambulance arrives is trained in first aid. What you aren't told is that he is also a vampire and that the blood seeping from your wound will be difficult for him to resist. You have not been warned about the presence of another agenda - one that changes the picture dramatically.

In 2009 an activist think tank observed that both Hare and a person named Malte have "long been key members of the Greenpeace International climate team." Malte's surname is Meinshausen. In 2001 he and Hare co-authored an analysis of the Kyoto Protocol. During 2002 and 2003 he was a Greenpeace spokesperson. [note 6-1]

But these facts didn't prevent him from being recruited as a contributing author to not one, not two, but three chapters of the 2007 Climate Bible. Like the graduate students discussed above, Meinshausen's participation demonstrates that many IPCC authors are hardly elder scholars. He only received his doctorate in 2005.

A number of passages in the 2007 Climate Bible blandly cite research papers authored by Hare and Meinshausen as though it's immaterial that they are Greenpeace personnel. Indeed, the IPCC goes so far as to reprint a graph that appears in a paper for which these two men are the sole authors.

But the Greenpeace connection extends still further. Australian marine biologist Ove Hoegh-Guldberg is often described as a "world renowned reef expert." Nine chapters of the 2007 Climate Bible base their conclusions partly on his work. [note 6-2] He was a contributing author to that report and has been appointed a coordinating lead author for the upcoming edition.

The problem is that Hoegh-Guldberg has had close ties to activist organizations for the past 17 years. Between 1994 and 2000 he wrote four reports about coral reefs and climate change that were funded, vetted, and published by Greenpeace. Since then he has written two more for the World Wildlife Fund (WWF).

Someone who has spent 17 years working closely with activist groups is thoroughly tainted. By no stretch of the imagination can he be considered a disinterested party who will carefully weigh the pros and cons and then write a scrupulously objective account of the situation.

Speaking of the WWF, its website includes a formal photograph of 20 of the IPCC's most senior personnel. In the second row there's a gentleman named Richard Moss, who has been involved with the IPCC for nearly 20 years. During part of that time he was employed by the WWF as one of its vice-presidents. [note 6-3]

Similarly, Jennifer Morgan spent several years as the WWF's chief spokesperson on climate change. She led its global climate change program and headed its delegation to the Kyoto Protocol negotiations. Prior to that, she worked for the Climate Action Network. Currently she is director of a climate program for the World Resources Institute.

In other words, Morgan is not one of the world finest scientific minds. She is a professional activist. Yet in June 2010 the IPCC appointed her to work on a report it describes as objective, rigorous, and balanced.

Michael Oppenheimer is also worth a mention. When the public hears the term 'scientist' we think of someone who is above the fray - who's disinterested and dispassionate and who goes wherever the scientific results happen to lead. This implied neutrality is what gives scientists their authority. But in the 1970s a new kind of scientist began to emerge - the activist scientist. Nowadays these people occupy impressive positions at universities. They are often employed by respectable government bodies. All of that disguises the fact that they hold activist worldviews and that those views can influence their scientific judgment. [note 6-4]

Research findings are rarely clear-cut. Data is collected, selected, discarded, adjusted, and interpreted by human beings. At every juncture there is the risk of going astray, of dismissing information that is actually important. The bits and pieces that get left on the cutting-room floor might add up to a different story. Because activist scientists begin with a particular narrative in mind, they may be unconsciously blind to these other possibilities.

At first glance, Oppenheimer could hardly seem more eminent. He is director of a program in science, technology and environmental policy at Princeton University, as well as a professor in the atmospheric sciences department.

Prior to these appointments, however, Oppenheimer spent more than two decades as the chief scientist for the activist Environmental Defense Fund (EDF). That organization is so wealthy its list of staff experts includes more than 100 names.

Among them are seven attorneys, eight economists, and a vice-president of corporate sponsorships.

Although we are familiar with the idea that big business exerts an influence on public debates, most of us have overlooked the fact that there's also such a thing as big green. Groups like the EDF lobby ferociously to advance their particular perspective. They also hire people who provide their activist agenda with a veneer of scientific respectability. Even now, Oppenheimer continues to advise the EDF. This means that his professional life has been spent in an activist milieu.

The IPCC doesn't think that matters. His online biography says Oppenheimer has been "a long-time participant." He was a lead author for the 2007 edition of the Climate Bible, is serving as an even more senior author for the upcoming edition, and also helped the IPCC write a special report on "climate extremes and disasters." [note 6-5]

Perhaps one of the reasons the IPCC doesn't view Oppenheimer as irredeemably contaminated is because the scientific profession itself appears to have lost its bearings on such matters. Oppenheimer's Princeton bio further tells us that he:

> has been a member of several panels of the National Academy of Sciences and is now a member of the National Academies' Board on Energy and Environmental Studies. He is also...a Fellow of the American Association for the Advancement of Science.

The activist scientists who emerged in the 1970s have been working their way into high-status, leadership positions. Rather than keeping its distance from those whose careers have been associated with activism, the scientific establishment now honors, celebrates, and promotes such people.

But this has consequences. The public is supposed to accept the Climate Bible's findings because it is a scientific document written by the world's top scientific experts. What happens when the public discovers that those involved are actually brazen activists? What happens when it discovers that the world's most illustrious science bodies have themselves stopped drawing a line in the sand between activists and those who strive to pursue science in a genuinely neutral and unbiased fashion?

If scientists want us to trust their expert opinions they need to behave in a trustworthy manner. If they want us to be impressed by their high standards, they need to enforce these standards.

From this perspective, the shenanigans at the IPCC shed light on a broader malaise within the scientific community as a whole.

7 – CLIMATE MODELERS

Along with graduate students, those appointed due to their gender or their county, and activists, yet another group is prominent among IPCC authors - climate modelers. Although these people are often called *scientists*, their work has little in common with traditional science.

The scientific method involves forming an hypothesis, testing that hypothesis in the real world, and then confirming, adjusting, or abandoning the hypothesis according to what the real-world tests reveal. But there is no duplicate planet Earth on which experiments may be safely conducted. No one knows, therefore, what will happen if the number of carbon dioxide molecules in the atmosphere increases from 390 to 600 parts per million.

These really are the amounts under discussion. Scientists believe carbon dioxide used to comprise less than 0.03% of the atmosphere - 280 parts per *million* - prior to the industrial revolution. Currently, at 390 parts per million, it's approaching 0.04%. Barring emissions reductions, by the year 2100 that number could reach 0.06%. All this fuss is based on a hypothesis that says our planet is so unstable a slight increase in one particular trace gas will trigger disaster. [note 7-1]

Since there's no way to actually test this hypothesis, some people have adopted an alternative approach. They say that supercomputers programmed with complex mathematical formulas confirm that a bit more CO_2 in the atmosphere will be really bad news. In the view of climate modelers, these computer *simulations* are as good as hard evidence.

But this requires a rather large leap of faith. If math and computing power were the only things necessary to predict the future, investors would already know the price at which gold will be trading five, ten, and twenty years hence. But the world is chaotic and unpredictable. It rarely unfolds in the manner that even the smartest people, aided by graphs, charts, and computers, think it will.

Many of the same institutions now involved in long-term climate modeling got their start predicting short-term weather. We all know how unreliable that can be. Sometimes the weather behaves the way the experts think it will. Often it does not.

Freeman Dyson, one of the world's most eminent physicists, has studied climate models. He says that although they do some things well,

> They do not begin to describe the real world that we live in. The real world is muddy and messy and full of things that we do not yet understand. It is much easier for a scientist to sit in an air-conditioned building and run computer models, than to put on winter clothes and measure what is really happening outside in the swamps and the clouds. That is why the climate model experts end up believing their own models.

In other words, climate modelers spend their professional lives in a virtual world rather than in the real one. If an engineer's bridge is faulty, it doesn't matter how highly his fellow engineers praise its design, harsh reality will make its shortcomings evident to everyone. Since climate modelers are insulated from real world checks-and-balances (there's no way to verify their long term predictions in the short term), the only thing that seems to matter are the opinions of other modelers. This is a recipe for tunnel-vision. It is groupthink waiting to happen.

The research bodies that fund climate modeling teams don't appear to have taken any precautions against groupthink. Nor has the IPCC subjected climate models to rigorous evaluation by neutral, disinterested parties. Instead, it recruits the same people who work with these models on a daily basis to write the section of the Climate Bible that passes judgment on them. This is like asking parents to rate their own children's attractiveness. Do we really expect them to tell us their kids are homely?

The relationship between one country's climate modelers and the IPCC illustrates this point. George Boer is considered the architect of Canada's climate modeling efforts. As an employee of Environment Canada (which also produces weather forecasts), he has spent much of his career attempting to convince the powers-that-be that climate models are a legitimate use of public money. There has been a direct relationship between how persuasive he has been and how many staff he's been permitted to hire, how much computing power he's been permitted to purchase, and the amount of professional prestige he has acquired.

Given that his own interests are closely linked to the effectiveness with which he *promotes* climate models, he is emphatically not the sort of person who's likely to conduct the cold, hard assessment the public is entitled to expect before the entire world begins taking climate model results seriously.

Nevertheless, when the IPCC chose 10 lead authors to write a chapter titled *Climate Models - Evaluation* for its 1995 edition, Boer was among them. So was Andrew Weaver, another Canadian whose entire career depends on climate modeling. (The term 'climate modeler' would seem to apply to a minimum of five of that chapter's other eight lead authors.)

When the same chapter of the 2001 edition of the Climate Bible got written, the story was similar. Weaver and two other modelers repeated their lead author roles. Boer, along with four other Canadians who earn their living as climate modelers, all served as contributing authors.

By the time the IPCC published the 2007 Climate Bible, had it realized that asking climate modelers to evaluate their own handiwork was foolhardy? Nope. Climate modelers once again comprised the vast majority of lead authors for the *Climate Models and Their Evaluation* chapter.

I'm sure that all of those currently involved in writing the *Evaluation of Climate Models* chapter of the upcoming Climate Bible are marvelous human beings. But if the world were to decide that climate models are a colossal waste of time and money, many of them would be out of a job. How likely is it, therefore, that this chapter will come to such a conclusion?

In other words, nothing like an independent assessment of the strengths and weaknesses of these models is actually taking place.

But the story gets worse. Climate modelers also write other sections of the Climate Bible - including the crucial *attribution* chapter. This is where the most important question of all gets decided: Is the slight recent warming of the planet due to human activity or is it part of a perfectly natural, ongoing cycle of both warming and cooling?

For the IPCC's 2007 report, the two most senior authors of that chapter – Gabriele Hegerl and Francis Zwiers – were both climate modelers. They based their decision on what they believe their models reveal. [note 7-2]

The IPCC may claim that the world's top scientific minds and climate modelers are one and the same. But I think that's a stretch. In July 2007, five IPCC authors wrote an article for *Scientific American* in which they equated climate models with a fortune-teller's crystal ball.

On the one hand, they declared it a certainty that people, plants, and animals would all be living with the consequences of human-induced climate change "for at least the next thousand years." On the other, they said:

> Unfortunately, the crystal ball provided by our climate models becomes cloudier for predictions out beyond a century or so.

Each of us has to make up our own mind regarding whom to trust and what to believe. But when I became a grownup, I stopped believing in crystal balls.

8 – CLEAR AS MUD

Because window panes are transparent, we can see through them. But a window into which no one bothers to peer can become so splattered with mud that it turns opaque. The people on the other side of the window, the insiders, may not notice the state of the glass. They may sincerely believe all is well.

When the committee that examined IPCC policies and procedures posted a questionnaire on its website, those with direct experience of that organization were given an opportunity to voice their concerns. Outsiders also got a chance to express theirs. Surprisingly, both groups reported large amounts of mud. It turns out that few people understand how the IPCC makes some of its most important decisions.

This is an embarrassing revelation. For years, IPCC leaders have boasted that this organization is a model of transparency. According to them, it's one of the reasons we should have faith in IPCC findings.

In 2007 chairman Pachauri told a newspaper: "So you can't think of a more transparent process...than what we have in the IPCC." In 2009 he insisted in a magazine interview: "The IPCC is a totally transparent organization...Whatever we do is available for scrutiny at every stage."

In early 2010, when more than 250 US scientists signed an open letter defending the IPCC, the letter declared: "We conclude that the IPCC procedures are transparent and thorough..."

But there's the party line and then there are the experiences of real people. The person whose remarks begin on page three of the collected questionnaire answers is not an IPCC novice. He or she has been a contributing author, a lead author, and even a coordinating lead author. Yet, when asked to comment on how the IPCC selects its lead authors, this person says: "I'm not clear how this actually happens..."

As it turns out, such confusion is widespread among IPCC insiders. In answering this question these people used words such as *mysterious*, *closed-door*, and *black box*. They said things like:

- Selection of lead authors in my view is the most important decision in the IPCC process, and it is not transparent. (p. 185)
- After being [either a lead author or a coordinating lead author] several times, I still have no idea how I was selected. This is unacceptable. (p. 180)
- It has always been unclear how this has been undertaken... (p. 126)

None of this makes the IPCC look good.

Doing a poor job of explaining how things work isn't a crime. Many large organizations no doubt do this equally badly. The problem is that the IPCC told us this was a yardstick by which its credibility should be judged. Again and again, we've been told it excels at transparency. But it does not.

In fact, Climate Bible authors are chosen via a secretive process. First, the IPCC receives nominations from governments - but it declines to make public the names of these nominees. Second, the IPCC fails to explain what selection criteria it uses. Third, when it announces who has been chosen, the only piece of information it feels obliged to provide is the name of the country the author represents. [note 8-1]

In what other context, when a hiring announcement is made, is a person's nationality announced yet no mention is made of their specific credentials?

We know that authors' resumes are submitted as part of the nomination process - but they are then locked in a drawer. It would be easy for the IPCC to post these resumes on its website, but it chooses not to.

In other words, an organization that claims to be utterly transparent expects us to simply take it on faith that the most qualified people were nominated and selected. Moreover, it feels no obligation to provide the slightest bit of evidence that those who got the job are, in fact, experts.

When the committee that posted the online questionnaire delivered its own report in August 2010, it said the IPCC lacks transparency in other areas, as well. For example, it's far from clear what criteria the IPCC uses when deciding who should fill senior management positions. Moreover, while a general outline is drawn up by a small group of individuals before a new Climate Bible gets underway, those who aren't invited to take part in this step have no idea how this happens – or who is involved.

While the IPCC is supposed to survey the scientific literature, it has never supplied its authors (remember, some of them are in their 20s) with guidelines as to how to complete this task. The manner in which this has occurred over the past two decades is, therefore, anyone's guess – a situation rather opposite to complete transparency.

The IPCC's transparency shortcomings have been obvious for some time. In 2005 Steve McIntyre, a Canadian with a Masters degree in mathematics and a flair for statistics, was invited by the IPCC to be an expert reviewer for what would become the 2007 edition of the Climate Bible. McIntyre, who writes the ClimateAudit.org blog, was by then a well-known IPCC critic, so this invitation was a promising sign. But it didn't take long for matters to go off the rails.

McIntyre noticed that, in a particular section of the report, the IPCC was basing its arguments on two research papers that hadn't yet been published. In itself, this should ring alarm bells. Since the wider scientific community had been given no opportunity to scrutinize them, it was surely premature to consider them solid pieces of evidence.

McIntyre asked to examine the underlying data associated with these two papers. Since IPCC rules say it's the job of its technical support units to provide expert reviewers with material that isn't readily available, he contacted the head of the appropriate unit. That gentleman's name is Martin Manning. An atmospheric scientist who now heads a research institute at a New Zealand university, Manning is one of the authors of the *Scientific American* article that refers to crystal balls.

He refused - not once, but twice - to help McIntyre. This is what his second e-mail said:

> Let me repeat – If you wish to obtain data used in a paper then you should make a direct request to the original authors yourself. It would be inappropriate for the IPCC to become involved in that communication and I have no intention of allowing the IPCC support unit to provide you with what would in effect be a secretarial service. There are over 1200 other scientists on our list of reviewers and we simply can not get involved in providing special services for each...I will not be responding to further correspondence on this matter.

One would think that a scientifically rigorous organization would go to some effort to ensure that its expert reviewers (all of whom, by the way, volunteer their time) have access to all the information necessary for them to make an informed judgment. One would also think that whenever the IPCC chooses to rely on as-yet-unpublished papers it would welcome the fact that someone was offering to take a close look at the data on which such papers are based. The Climate Bible isn't just any report, after all. It informs the decisions of governments around the world.

Shortly afterward, McIntyre sent two e-mails, dated a few days apart, to Susan Solomon. In 2008 *Time* magazine named this US atmospheric chemist one of the world's 100 most influential people largely due to her senior role in assembling the 2007 Climate Bible. McIntyre told Solomon that Manning had declined to help him. He also reported a far more shocking development. Both authors had subsequently refused to cooperate. One said the underlying data would only be released after the paper had been published. The other advised him to contact the journal to which the second paper had been submitted.

Solomon's own response could hardly have been less helpful. IPCC rules, she said, only oblige the technical support units to provide copies of unpublished papers themselves. The IPCC does not, said Solomon, concern itself with the raw data on which papers - published or otherwise - are based.

In a bizarre turn of events Solomon then accused McIntyre of behaving improperly. By contacting the journal as he'd been advised to, she said McIntyre was interfering with that journal's internal decisions. She also claimed it was inappropriate for him to suggest to the journal that his role as an IPCC reviewer entitled him to examine this data.

In her capacity as a high-profile member of a body that claims to be *totally transparent* Solomon took the strange position that the unpublished papers were confidential material. As an IPCC reviewer, McIntyre had been granted access to them for one purpose only: to read them. By seeking more information, she said, he was violating IPCC confidentiality provisions and therefore risked being struck from the IPCC's list of official reviewers:

> we must insist that from now on you honor all conditions of access to unpublished, and therefore confidential, material...The IPCC rules...have served the scientific and policy communities well for numerous past international assessment rounds. If there is further evidence that you can not accept them, or if your intent is to...challenge them, then we will not be able to continue to treat you as an expert reviewer for the IPCC.

This organization says it welcomes scrutiny, but actions speak louder than words. Rather than embracing inquiring minds, it threatens them with expulsion. As a commenter on McIntyre's blog aptly observed, it would seem that IPCC reviewers are supposed to behave like rubber stamps rather than microscopes.

The IPCC's leadership - represented by Solomon and Manning - failed more than a transparency test here. Solomon had a choice. If safeguarding the integrity of the IPCC was her top concern, she should have scolded the authors of the papers who were refusing to let McIntyre double-check their work. She should have advised them that the IPCC would exclude their papers from consideration unless they made their data available immediately.

Instead, Solomon behaved like a bureaucrat. Rather than championing openness, rather than behaving as though important questions affecting the entire planet were at stake, she chose to defend individual researchers' pre-publication confidentiality concerns.

It's worth noting that the author who refused outright to make her data available prior to her paper's final publication was Gabriele Hegerl. You may remember her name from the climate model discussion earlier.

Hegerl isn't just anyone. Rather, she served in seven distinct capacities with regard to the 2007 Climate Bible. Significantly, she was one of the two most senior people in charge of the attribution chapter - the section that decides the degree to which human influence versus natural causes are at work.

In other words, the IPCC entrusted the most central question of all to the judgment of a person it was fully aware had declined to share her data with one of its own expert reviewers. It has never had the grace (or the wisdom) to be the least bit embarrassed about this.

Here's how Solomon could have convinced me that the IPCC is an honorable organization: She could have rebuked the authors of these two papers and then issued an IPCC-wide memo announcing that she had done so. She could have declared that refusing to share one's data amounts to scientific malpractice and that the IPCC would no longer pay attention to research produced by people who behave in this manner. She could have instructed the technical support units to lend every assistance to expert reviewers seeking additional information - inviting anyone who encountered difficulties in that regard to contact her directly.

When the IPCC wonders why people don't trust it, it need look no further than the fact that nothing remotely like this occurred.

9 – THE IMMENSE EDIFICE THAT WASN'T

Many people believe the IPCC goes to the trouble of verifying the research on which it bases its conclusions. An oft-repeated quote from President Barack Obama's science advisor, John Holdren, is a marvelous example of this. Holdren says the IPCC is the source of "the most important conclusions" about climate change, and that these conclusions rest on:

> ...an immense edifice of painstaking studies published in the world's leading peer-reviewed scientific journals. **They have been vetted** and documented **in excruciating detail** by the largest, longest, costliest, most international, most interdisciplinary, and most thorough formal review of a scientific topic ever conducted. [bold added]

Here's a similar quote, from climate modeler Richard Rood:

> The scientists who write the IPCC reports use exquisite rigor...the result is a document which is based on the facts...which have been scrutinized to the highest level possible.

But as we have discovered, the IPCC takes research findings at face value. It doesn't double-check that the raw data actually shows what a researcher claims it does. It feels no need to look under the hood - and discourages its expert reviewers from doing so. Holdren and Rood are therefore mistaken. The IPCC does not scrutinize the facts on which it relies. It performs no vetting whatsoever - never mind the sort that could be described as excruciatingly detailed.

When IPCC insiders were asked for their thoughts about quality assurance, their questionnaire answers confirmed this. Here are some of their verbatim remarks:

- As far as I can tell, there is no data quality assurance associated with what the IPCC is doing... (p. 99)
- Since the IPCC is a review body, it does not do data assurance or quality control in a systematic fashion. (p. 52)
- Quality assurance and error identification is not existent... (p. 384)
- Data quality assurance, per se, is beyond the scope of the work of the IPCC... (p. 203)

Many of these individuals said the IPCC should not be held responsible for the accuracy of statements that appear in research papers it cites since "that is an issue for the journals concerned." In the words of someone else, "it is expected that a paper published in an important journal" has already received a quality assurance check.

Other IPCC insiders, however, recognize the shortcomings of this approach. There are thousands of journals out there, but no accreditation process to ensure their quality. How smart is it, therefore, to blindly assume that a published paper is an accurate paper? As one person observed, some research merely makes an interesting contribution to the 'intellectual conversation' (p. 332). That standard is surely far too low to justify an IPCC conclusion.

Once we understand a few other relevant facts, Holdren's claimed edifice crumbles entirely. Academic journals make use of a quality-control mechanism called peer review. The general idea is that, when a paper is submitted to a journal in the hope that it will be published, it gets assigned to an employee of the journal called an editor. The editor sends copies of the paper to reviewers presumed to be knowledgeable about the topic under discussion.

Generally speaking, there are three reviewers whose identities remain anonymous even after the paper is published. Sometimes these reviewers are called referees. Although the reviewers look over the paper it is important to appreciate that, in many cases, only the most cursory of assessments takes place. In the words of one senior scientist:

> A reviewer is normally not paid for his work. With the best will in the world, he is able to spend no more than a few hours examining any particular manuscript. He is able to do little more than see that the story being told is superficially coherent and makes no obvious errors of fact. [note 9-1]

If the reviewers have concerns, they tell the editor about them - who then asks the paper's author for a response. Sometimes a paper will undergo a major re-write before the editor is satisfied it is fit for publication. But this does not mean its conclusions are correct. Far from it. Richard Horton, the editor of *The Lancet* medical journal, argues this point forcefully:

> Peer review does not prove that a piece of research is true. The best it can do is say that, on the basis of a written account of what was done and some interrogation of the authors, the research seems on the face of it to be acceptable for publication...Experience shows, for example, that peer review is an extremely unreliable way to detect research misconduct.

A recent commentary titled *The Peer Review Fetish* makes a similar point:

> A couple reviewers, of course, are a poor substitute for mass scrutiny. Sometimes reviewers are chosen poorly; other times they're lazy.

...Conflating peer review with scientific soundness impoverishes our appreciation of the scientific process. Peer review should be one criterion that people use in assessing the strength of any given piece of research – nothing more, nothing less.

What this all adds up to is that the only time research findings can be considered valid is if someone else, working entirely independently, follows the same procedures as those described in the paper and arrives at the same result. There used to be perfect clarity in the scientific community that unless a piece of research had passed that kind of test, it should be viewed with caution. Based on McIntyre's experience with the two unpublished papers discussed above, it appears the IPCC now regards research as reliable long before it has even appeared in print.

When one remembers that a great deal of climate research involves computer modeling (employing millions of lines of computer code), there's another reason for concern. As geophysics professor Jon Claerbout points out:

An article about computational science in a scientific publication isn't the scholarship itself, it's **merely advertising**...The actual scholarship is the complete software development environment and the complete set of instructions which generated the figures. [bold added] [note 9-2]

Peer-reviewers don't get within a mile of climate modeling supercomputers and their software. Which means they have no realistic way of evaluating entire categories of research papers that are central to the IPCC's analysis. All a peer-reviewer can do is assess the advertising - the portions of the story the climate modeler chooses to discuss in his or her paper.

Phil Jones, one of the world's most prominent climatologists, has published in the most prestigious journals. When he testified before a UK parliamentary committee early in 2010, he was asked how often peer reviewers had sought to examine his raw data and computer codes. "They've never asked," he replied.

While we're on the subject of quality assurance, IPCC insiders who answered the questionnaire identified another weak link. A great deal of climate research involves huge collections of data - such as temperature records from thousands of locations stretching back scores of years. But the accuracy of these numbers has never been verified by independent personnel. As one IPCC insider observed, academic journals may consider unverified data good enough - but quality control mechanisms surely need to be in place before the IPCC relies on such data to make real-world decisions. [note 9-3]

Let us return to that quote from presidential advisor John Holdren. He says the IPCC's conclusions are the result of the most thorough formal review of a scientific topic ever conducted. How can this be the case when the IPCC hasn't bothered to verify the temperature data on which so much of climate science rests?

Would an auditor approve a company's financial statements before confirming the accuracy of the underlying numbers?

10 – THE SHIELD AND THE SWORD

The IPCC boasts about peer-reviewed studies the same way it boasts about transparency. We're told we should trust the Climate Bible because it isn't based on just any research - but on peer-reviewed research. This is intended to wow us. According to the marketing spin, the world knows human-caused climate change is underway because the IPCC has consulted mountains of peer-reviewed scientific papers.

Journalists fell for this hook, line, and sinker. Seth Borenstein, a science writer with the Associated Press, covers the IPCC extensively. Because he works for a newswire service, the stories he writes often appear on the front pages of national newspapers as well as in numerous smaller publications. During the year 2007 Borenstein repeatedly told his readers that the IPCC relies on peer-reviewed scientific literature. [note 10-1]

The science editor of the *Times* of London also did so. So has *The Economist* magazine, Australia's publicly-funded broadcaster, the bulletin of the International Atomic Energy Agency, and Ireland's *Independent* newspaper.

In none of these instances did the journalist mention that peer review in no way ensures truth - or that it is often perfunctory in nature. That would have undermined the reason for alluding to it in the first place - which was to make the IPCC appear authoritative.

But that's only the beginning of the peer review tale. Bursting with bravado, this spoiled child of an organization pushed the envelope still further. In its zeal to persuade us that its findings are credible, the IPCC has spent years claiming it relies *only* on peer-reviewed literature.

In 2008, IPCC chairman Rajendra Pachauri addressed a committee of the North Carolina legislature. Here's what he said to those assembled law-makers:

> ...we carry out an assessment of climate change based on peer-reviewed literature, so **everything** that we look at and take into account in our assessments has to carry [the] credibility of peer-reviewed publications, **we don't settle for anything less than that.** [bold added]

In 2009 a journalist asked Pachauri whether the IPCC's next report would take into account a discussion paper issued by India's environment ministry that questioned the idea that Himalayan glaciers are endangered by climate change. Pachauri's response was arrogantly dismissive. The "IPCC studies only peer-review science," he said. "Let someone publish the data in a decent credible publication...otherwise we can just throw it into the dustbin."

The outright claim (or the implicit suggestion) that every last bit of evidence considered by the IPCC has met the peer-reviewed threshold has been repeated far and wide. Journalists have had a hand in this. So have governments and scientists.

The *Earth Negotiations Bulletin* describes itself as a "a balanced, timely and independent reporting service" that tracks the twists and turns of UN climate talks. Over the years it has received funding from numerous countries including Australia, Canada, Germany, France, Italy, Spain, the UK, and the United States. Between 2001 and 2010 this bulletin sounded a constant refrain. Again and again, as part of its boilerplate description, it told its readers that IPCC reports are based on "peer-reviewed scientific and technical literature."

For its part, the US National Oceanic and Atmospheric Administration (NOAA) celebrated the role its employees had played in the Nobel Prize-winning IPCC by devoting a page to that topic in an official publication. Its description of the IPCC makes a point of mentioning that it relies on "published peer-reviewed literature." A bit more of the commentary from that page sheds light on how our delinquent teenager got to be quite so impressed with himself. According to this government publication:

> The IPCC Assessments, internationally recognized as the premier source about climate change, are used by scientists and policy makers worldwide...The IPCC relies on world-class scientists from 113 governments to scour and evaluate the body of scientific literature on climate science.

Sounds great, doesn't it? Until you discover that *world-class scientists* include 20-something graduate students. Until you learn that the IPCC prevents expert reviewers from looking too closely at the science. (Incidentally, the NOAA publication proudly mentions one staff member in particular - Susan Solomon, the very person who threatened to expel Steve McIntyre because he'd asked for more information.)

While journalists and bureaucrats may be prone to exaggeration, scientists are supposed to refrain from making declarative statements about matters beyond their firsthand knowledge. Nevertheless scientists themselves have actively promoted the peer-reviewed meme.

In 2006 Andrew Dessler, a Texas professor who specializes in the physics of climate change, declared (on a website) that the public shouldn't consult websites when seeking global warming information since, unlike IPCC reports, they weren't "based entirely on peer-reviewed literature."

In 2008 physicist Joseph Romm, writing under a headline that promised *The cold truth about climate change*, told Salon.com readers that the IPCC "relies on the peer-reviewed scientific literature for its conclusions, which must meet the rigorous requirements of the scientific method..."

In 2009 Greenpeace-linked marine biologist Ove Hoegh-Guldberg described the IPCC process to a reporter as "always using the peer-reviewed literature as the base." Philip Duffy, a physicist with 20 years climate modeling experience, asserted in 2010 that a "core principle of the IPCC is that only peer-reviewed literature is cited."

In other words, peer review has become both a shield (behind which the IPCC hides) and a sword (with which it skewers dissenting voices). Anyone who attempts to challenge IPCC findings is told to go read the peer-reviewed literature. Moreover, unless a criticism has been published in a peer-reviewed journal IPCC-affiliated scientists consider it beneath their notice.

In 2003 climatologist Michael Mann was asked to respond to concerns expressed in an article written by a former US Defense and Energy Secretary and published in a major newspaper. Much like Chairman Pachauri - who said that research that hadn't appeared in a journal was fit only for the dustbin - Mann haughtily replied: "I am not familiar with any peer-reviewed work that he has submitted to the scientific literature."

In 2011, the following tagline appeared beneath an opinion piece published in an Australian newspaper: *Cathy Foley is president of Science & Technology Australia, Australia's peak body for science and technology. She has had 82 refereed papers published in international journals.*

In that opinion piece Foley declared that a climate skeptic then on a speaking tour in her country would lack credibility "until he is willing to subject his views to the rigorous peer review process." He shouldn't be listened to, she said, because he:

> has never published a single peer-reviewed paper on any scientific topic in his life...The challenge for him is to test his ideas by submitting them to the robust peer-review process. It's a method that has operated for hundreds of years providing the community with **information that it can trust**. [bold added]

Since Al Gore hasn't published any peer-reviewed papers either, it would be interesting to know whether Foley has similarly declared his credibility to be nil during his speaking tours. Having evidently missed the editor of *The Lancet*'s remarks about how peer review fails to detect research misconduct, she ended her piece by urging Australians to "respect the peer-reviewed science."

11 – THE PEER REVIEW FAIRY TALE

Having repeatedly encountered the claim that IPCC reports rely solely on peer-reviewed literature, in early 2010 I was taken aback by a blog post authored by economist Richard Tol. He complained that, in a particular chapter of the 2007 Climate Bible, IPCC authors had ignored the findings of peer-reviewed studies and had instead cited non-peer-reviewed material to make the opposite case.

Looking up that chapter's list of references online, I wondered how this could be. And yet, as I began to scan these references for the first time, I discovered the IPCC had relied on numerous sources that had not, in fact, been published in scientific journals.

It turns out the *we-use-only-peer-reviewed-scientific-literature* claim is total nonsense. It turns out those North Carolina legislators were misled by the head of the IPCC himself.

At that point in time I had no idea how large the discrepancy between the IPCC's marketing message and reality actually was. I just knew something smelled.

It's important to appreciate that the 2007 edition of the Climate Bible had been around for three years by then. There had been ample opportunity for any journalist - particularly those who write exclusively about science or the environment - to do some rudimentary fact-checking. This isn't hard. The full report is readily accessible on the Internet. But it seems no one had ever bothered.

I counted the references in the chapter Tol had mentioned. Next I split them into two groups: journal articles and everything else. Non-peer-reviewed material is often called *grey literature* and it seemed to me there were 139 in this category. That meant only 58% of the source material had come from peer-reviewed publications. This is a long way from 100%. Anyone who thinks it isn't should keep only 58% of their next paycheque and donate the remainder to charity.

Entirely at random I chose another chapter and performed a similar examination. To my astonishment, of the 260 references listed in that instance only 64 were to journal articles. Twenty-five percent. At that point I sat back in my chair, took off my glasses, and rubbed my eyes. What was going on? Had I accidently found the two chapters of the 2007 Climate Bible (out of a total of 44) that were outliers? Or was the problem more widespread?

Wondering whether anyone else had noticed the shockingly low percentage of peer-reviewed sources in this second chapter, I did something else for the first time. I went looking for the comments IPCC expert reviewers had submitted after reading early versions of this chapter. Had they spotted this problem?

It turns out this matter had, in fact, been raised. But the IPCC shrugged it off.

These reviewer comments, paired with responses from IPCC authors, suggest that everyone was taking part in a shared hallucination. A great deal of lip service got paid to peer review, but in practice it was a next-to-meaningless concept.

When Takayuki Takeshita, a researcher associated with the University of Tokyo, suggested that a presentation he'd helped prepare be taken into account, IPCC authors told him it was ineligible since it didn't satisfy the requirement that sources be published. But if these authors really cared about the rules, three out of four of that chapter's references would never have made the cut.

Elsewhere, when Takeshita said he considered an assertion in the chapter to be "doubtful" and noted that it conflicted with almost "all of the literature I have ever read," he was told: "Rejected; text simply quotes the study, and good chance the study is correct."

Did you catch that? Despite the fact that the study in question wasn't peer-reviewed, the IPCC authors thought there was a "good chance" it was correct – and that was the end of the matter.

On two separate occasions, another expert reviewer, John Kessels from the Energy Research Center of the Netherlands, complained that press releases were being cited to support statements of fact. "[I]s a press release scientific literature?" he asked. When the final version of the 2007 Climate Bible appeared, the press releases remained.

It had now become clear to me that an audit of all 44 chapters of the Climate Bible needed to be undertaken. The list of references appearing at the end of each one had to be examined. It was important to know just how many were actually peer-reviewed. But since some chapters list 400 or more references, and a few list 800 or more, the job was too large for one person. I needed help.

The Internet is a powerful and amazing invention. On March 8th, 2010 I wrote a blog post asking for assistance. The rules were simple. The references appearing at the end of each IPCC chapter would be examined by three people, working independently. They'd identify the non-peer-reviewed entries, tally them up, and calculate the percentages.

In the event that their findings differed slightly (the IPCC doesn't always include complete information, and it's difficult to tell whether some journals are peer-reviewed or not), the result most favorable to the IPCC would be used. Where there was uncertainty, the IPCC would receive the benefit-of-the-doubt. This wasn't about nitpicking. What mattered was the big picture.

Within hours, I began receiving offers of assistance from people around the world. A surgeon from Kentucky. A night-shift worker from Australia. A software whiz from Vancouver. A retired engineer from Germany. Soon, more than 40 individuals from 12 countries had been in touch and a four-week dash to the finish line had begun.

Ordinary people volunteered many hours of their personal time to this project, which I called the Citizen Audit. In a handful of cases, fearing negative repercussions in their workplace or communities, they asked not to be publicly identified. One man told me that his neighbors might slash his tires or set fire to his house.

Think about that. What kind of moment in history do we inhabit when people feel that helping to fact-check a UN document places them at risk? In an era in which freedom of thought, religion, and speech are supposed to be valued why should counting up references in the Climate Bible be the slightest bit controversial?

After the results were all in, a few more days were required to do the math, write a brief report, and compile some tables. Five weeks later, on April 14th, we made our results public. Of the 18,531 references in the 2007 Climate Bible we found 5,587 - a full 30% - to be non peer-reviewed. The peer review score was so low in 21 out of 44 instances, the chapter would have received an F on an elementary school report card (59% or less).

Among the sources used to support IPCC assertions were newspaper and magazine articles, unpublished Masters and doctoral theses, Greenpeace and World Wildlife Fund documents, and yes, press releases.

While Chairman Pachauri had declared an Indian government discussion paper fit only for the dustbin, we found that the Climate Bible cites dozens of discussion papers. In one case, the document relied on by the IPCC was clearly labeled as 'version one' of a *draft*.

I wish I could say the release of our findings triggered a media frenzy, that journalists took notice and that this UN body was asked some tough questions. Such as:

- If the IPCC can't be trusted to describe it's own report accurately why should we believe anything else it says?
- How can the head of the IPCC be so misinformed?
- Does chairman Pachauri intend to set the record straight with those North Carolina legislators?

To my knowledge only one news outlet contacted the IPCC. A spokeswoman acknowledged the IPCC was aware of the Citizen Audit findings, but declined to comment.

Six days after we released our results, an article authored by Pachauri appeared in a Yale University online publication. It claimed the 2007 edition of the Climate Bible "cited approximately 18,000 peer-reviewed publications." We found less than 13,000.

It further said that "a limited amount of gray (or non-peer-reviewed) literature" had been cited "in cases where peer-reviewed literature was unavailable." Actually, this occurred 5,587 times. [note 11-1]

12 – FACTS AND FICTION

The responses provided by IPCC insiders to the online questionnaire make it clear large numbers of them were fully aware that the IPCC's use of non-peer-reviewed material is rampant. Question number five mentioned this material. Here are some verbatim remarks:

- The use of grey literature is unavoidable...Authors should not be plagued by unnecessary rules on the use or non-use of literature... (p. 622)
- My...chapter depended heavily on non-peer reviewed literature and I have yet to hear a complaint about its quality. (p. 52)
- If I take it that the role of IPCC is to sift available knowledge on climate-related [matters] to help policymakers then the use of grey literature is unavoidable ...It would be a ducking of responsibility to omit this literature... (p. 123)

Again and again, IPCC insiders used terms such *essential*, *necessary*, and *unavoidable* while discussing such material.

This means the chairman of the IPCC has a history of systematically misrepresenting the process by which his organization produces reports. His declaration that the IPCC *does not settle for anything less* than peer-reviewed sources is dead wrong. Nor is it wrong by a trivial amount. When 21 out of 44 chapters have so few peer-reviewed references they score an F, a serious disjuncture exists between the facts and the IPCC's fiction.

This raises an equally disturbing matter. It's abundantly clear numerous individuals knew Pachauri's public statements were at odds with reality. Hundreds – perhaps thousands – of people involved in the IPCC knew perfectly well he was misleading top government officials as well as the public every time he made the *we only use peer-reviewed sources* claim. Yet the average journalist, and therefore the average member of the public, remains in the dark.

In recent years, scientists affiliated with the IPCC have signed many open letters urging governments to pursue a variety of climate change measures. These letters have been published in newspapers and in journals. They have also been posted online. [note 12-1]

So where are the open letters, signed by hundreds of scientists, setting the record straight regarding the IPCC's use of grey literature? Why have there been no public declarations to the effect that while the undersigned support the work of the IPCC, not everything being said by the IPCC's leadership is borne out by the facts?

The willingness of everyone involved to overlook this discrepancy is further evidence that the IPCC is an outrageously spoiled child. No one expects it to follow the rules the rest of the world lives by. No one calls it onto the carpet when it tells tall tales. Keeping up the fiction of how admirable this child is has always been more important.

In other contexts, this would be called a conspiracy of silence. When people know that dramatic untruths are being uttered yet decline to challenge them, it means they belong to an organization that lacks integrity. A long, long list of IPCC officials flunked a basic test here. Like everyone else, they chose to avert their eyes.

But leadership failed on another level, as well. We are repeatedly told we should believe in dangerous, human-caused global warming because science academies from around the world have endorsed the IPCC's findings. Climate skeptics are frequently asked why they imagine their own judgment to be more reliable than the judgment of such esteemed bodies.

The answer to that question is this: No science academy noticed that one in three references in the 2007 Climate Bible is actually to grey literature. If these academies are so well-informed why did it take a group of Internet-linked volunteers to bring this to the world's attention? Why didn't even one of these science academies subject chairman Pachauri's rhetoric to rudimentary fact-checking?

If the world's science organizations had spent the past decade helping to keep the IPCC honest that would be one thing. f they had issued statements pointing out that the IPCC chairman was misleading the world about the nature of the IPCC's reports, they'd have earned my respect.

Instead, they've been just another group of godparents - standing shoulder-to-shoulder with this delinquent teen, smiling for the cameras, and giving him absolutely no reason to pull up his socks.

13 – SCREW THE RULES

According to the statement at OpenLetterFromScientists.com, there's nothing seriously amiss at the IPCC. There are rules, the rules get followed, therefore there's no problem. In the words of this letter:

> The impression that the IPCC does not have a proper quality-control procedure is deeply mistaken. The procedure for compiling reports and assuring its quality control is governed by well-documented principles that are reviewed regularly and amended as appropriate.

But take a close look at that quote. These scientists would have us believe that the fact that certain rules are *reviewed and amended regularly* proves they're actually being followed. This is the equivalent of suggesting that because speed limit signs get re-painted occasionally no one ever exceeds the limit.

But rules are meaningless if an organization lacks internal enforcement mechanisms. If there's no penalty for disregarding the rules, they may as well not exist.

Despite the fact that chairman Pachauri has spent years telling the world that IPCC reports are based solely on peer-reviewed literature, the IPCC actually had a policy which said grey literature could be cited at the discretion of chapter authors. This policy stated that, in such instances, the source material had to be clearly identified as non-peer-reviewed when it appeared in the list of references.

This would seem to be a reasonable compromise. If a document as influential as the Climate Bible is basing its conclusions on material that hasn't even been subject to academic peer review, surely it's appropriate to alert readers to this fact.

But most IPCC insiders were apparently unaware of this rule. Our Citizen Audit identified 5,587 non-peer-reviewed references. Hilary Ostrov, a Canadian blogger and one of these citizen auditors, conducted a global search and found that a grand total of six (or 0.1%) were flagged as such.

The InterAcademy Council (IAC) committee that investigated the IPCC also noticed this problem. In its words, a search of the Climate Bible "found few instances of information flagged" as non-peer-reviewed. [note 13-1]

Did any of the people who helped prepare the 2007 Climate Bible suffer any repercussions for violating this rule? Nada. Did any science academy shout from the rooftops that an organization that wants the entire world to trust its conclusions needs to faithfully follow its own policies? Fat chance.

Declaring that stronger enforcement mechanisms were needed, the IAC committee made a specific recommendation. It said the IPCC should "strengthen and enforce" its procedures so that, going forward, grey material would be "appropriately flagged" in its reports. [note 13-2]

In this respect, the committee was in harmony with some of the IPCC insiders who answered its online questionnaire. Some felt different colours should be used in IPCC reports "so one can immediately see without looking at the reference list whether the source for any piece of information is a peer-reviewed paper." Others suggested the use of italics or asterisks. [note 13-3] In the opinion of the person speaking on page 643:

References in the text to grey literature should be recognizable as grey, so that reviewers are alerted that the source is not peer reviewed. Peer reviewed and non-peer

> reviewed sources should be listed in separate sections in
> the list of references.

In other words, the committee - as well as a number of the IPCC's own insiders - thought this rule served an important function.

So how did the IPCC respond? Did it issue a statement telling its personnel there was a new sheriff in town and that this rule would henceforth be enforced? Are there signs that our spoiled child is ready to start behaving like a grownup?

Not anytime soon. In April 2011 blogger Ostrov noticed that an internal document was suggesting that the IPCC should abandon the flagging rule altogether. According to this document, the IPCC's administrative personnel felt it "would not be practical" to identify grey literature in reference lists. What should be so difficult about this task in an era in which everyone has personal computers was not explained. [note 13-4]

A month later, it was the preference of IPCC bureaucrats - rather than the clear recommendation of the committee that investigated the IPCC - that prevailed. A new policy for dealing with grey literature (which vaguely says IPCC authors should cite high quality literature and that peer-reviewed material should receive priority) was approved at an IPCC meeting. All mention of identifying grey literature has now vanished. [note 13-5]

Reading between the lines, and taking into account some of the other IPCC questionnaire responses, this is my best guess as to what occurred: I think the IPCC's small group of clerical, technical, and bureaucratic staff actually wield an immense amount of power. They're the ones who live and breathe this organization. They understand better than anyone else how it works, and how easily a group of international delegates who meet only periodically can be led in certain directions.

Despite the fact that the IPCC rulebook said grey literature had to be clearly identified, I suspect the bureaucrats were always of the opinion that doing so was too much of a bother. So they simply ignored that requirement.

After the IPCC was publicly called on the carpet about this matter the bureaucrats, rather than finally complying with the rule, arranged for it to disappear. Making use of perfectly legitimate internal mechanisms, they proposed a new policy that simply left that part out.

The fact that the delegates at a large IPCC meeting then adopted this new policy tells us a great deal. It announces, on a flashing neon sign, that there are no consequences for breaking IPCC rules.

Should anyone have the bad manners to insist that rules are meant to be followed, never fear. They'll be out-maneuvered.

14 – THE STERN REVIEW SCANDAL

According to the previously-mentioned statement at Open-LetterFromScientists.com, the writing of the Climate Bible follows an orderly process. The first draft is commented on by expert reviewers, whose views are incorporated. Reviewers are then invited to comment on the second draft, and their remarks are taken into account. Eventually, the final version of the report is approved at a large meeting.

This sounds great in theory, but as we have already seen, IPCC authors are under no obligation to pay attention to expert reviewers. When Takayuki Takeshita told the IPCC it was making a claim that conflicted with virtually everything he'd read, he was blown off, his genuine concern dismissed by an IPCC author who thought there was a "good chance" the study being relied on was correct. When John Kessels told the IPCC it was inappropriate to rely on press releases for factual data, he too was waved aside.

Why do some people still believe that all is well in the land of the IPCC? I think it's helpful to recognize that this organization is, indeed, a bureaucracy. Bureaucracies excel at going through the motions. Even when these motions make little sense, even when they don't accomplish what they claim to be accomplishing, the bureaucratically-minded point to this busywork as proof that things are on track.

It's true that thousands of expert reviewers were invited to offer comments on two draft versions of the 2007 Climate Bible. It's also true that each comment was responded to by an IPCC author. But the fact that these authors are at perfect liberty to ignore perspectives that differ from their own means the entire purpose of this exercise (to spot errors and avoid groupthink) is fatally undermined. In reality, a lot of people's time is being wasted so the IPCC can *appear* to be rigorous and inclusive.

While the IPCC's marketing message talks constantly about the thousands of expert reviewers who take part, if one looks closely it's difficult not to conclude that the IPCC holds its expert reviewers in contempt.

An excellent example is the way the Stern Review was handled by the IPCC. This 700-page report was written by a team of UK government economists led by Nicholas Stern. In early 2007, just prior to the release of the second install-ment of what was then the IPCC's brand new Climate Bible, chairman Pachauri was interviewed by a reporter from the Bloomberg news service.

When asked whether the Climate Bible had relied on the Stern Review, Pachauri said that although his organiza-tion was aware of it, the IPCC's ability to make use of this document was limited because it wasn't peer-reviewed.

Imagine my surprise therefore when, during the Citizen Audit, I discovered that the IPCC had, in fact, cited the Stern Review all over the place. Not once or twice. And not in a chapter or two. We're talking at least 26 times across 12 chap-ters.

Since Pachauri had told Bloomberg that relying on this report would be improper why did the IPCC cite it so fre-quently - sometimes twice and, in one instance, *five* times on a single page? I mean, how much more heavily could the IPCC have leaned on the Stern Review *had* it been fully peer-reviewed? When the IPCC declared that three-quarters of a billion people in India and China depend on glaciers for their water supply, is it not strange that its only source for this claim was the Stern Review?

The concern here isn't just that the IPCC chairman ap-pears, once again, to have been clueless regarding the contents of his organization's premiere report. The far more serious problem is that the expert review process had already wrapped up before the Stern Review became available.

Reviewers examining the sections of the Climate Bible that cite the Stern Review were required to submit their comments by certain deadlines. In one case the deadline was July 21st, 2006. In the other it was September 15th.

This means the IPCC's expert reviewers had all gone home before the Stern Review was released at the end of October 2006. None of those references to the Stern Review were part of any draft the IPCC showed the 2,500 expert reviewers about whom Pachauri frequently boasts. They were quietly inserted into the Climate Bible *afterward*.

This raises some troubling questions:

- Why bother with expert reviewers if, after they're out of the picture, you going to add new material to 12 different chapters?
- If IPCC procedures are so airtight, if the people in charge of the IPCC have such integrity, how could this possibly have happened?
- How do we know that similar insertions of other new material didn't also take place?

It would appear that the relationship the IPCC has with its expert reviewers borders on the abusive. First it asks these people to volunteer their time in good faith. Then it gives its authors the right to dismiss their input with nothing more than a single word: *rejected*.

While expert reviewers are expected to comply with the IPCC's deadlines, this organization feels no need to respect such deadlines itself. Instead, it nonchalantly adds in, after the fact, arguments and source material these reviewers had no opportunity to assess.

Finally, for the icing on this sad little cake, the IPCC continues to use these expert reviewers as cover. Again and again, it points to its army of expert reviewers as evidence of how rigorous and trustworthy it is.

15 – CUTOFF DATES, WHAT CUTOFF DATES?

By now it has become clear that following its own procedures is not something the IPCC does well. I'm sorry to be repetitive but the obvious reason for this is that it has never appointed anyone to enforce them. Since no one has ever suffered any consequences for breaking the rules, it would be close to miraculous if they were actually being observed.

People involved in large projects who find themselves under time pressure tend to cut corners. This doesn't make them evil - it makes them human. If the IPCC were a truly vigilant organization its structure would take human failings into account. If the IPCC cared as much about quality control as the average factory, it would have personnel whose sole job is ensuring that standards are upheld.

Instead, the IPCC resembles a social club. In such a milieu people tend to look the other way when confronted with both large and small transgressions. Who needs the grief? If everyone around you is OK with the current arrangement, why rock the boat?

As we've already seen, no group of IPCC participants stepped forward to alert the public that Pachauri's 100% peer-reviewed claim was nonsense. If IPCC participants felt so little concern about this falsehood being uttered so frequently and openly, is it a surprise that the same people failed to object when they witnessed other moral lapses?

In April 2010, Pachauri wrote an article in which he attempted to defend the IPCC from critics. Trotting out his usual rhetoric about peer-reviewed publications, 2,500 expert reviewers, yada yada, he said he thought it important to explain how his organization functions. According to him, the 2007 Climate Bible "was based on scientific studies completed *before* January 2006, and did not include later studies" (my italics).

If we take Pachauri at his word, in order to be eligible for IPCC consideration research had to be available prior to 2006. But we know this cutoff date was a mirage because the Stern Review - a document that wasn't released until late 2006 - still made it in. It appears that when IPCC authors are intent on including certain material, they find a way to do so, cutoff dates or no cutoff dates.

The Climate Bible is really three smaller reports bundled together. The first, known as the Working Group 1 report, is where the hard science (if one is prepared to overlook the climate modeling aspect) is concentrated. This is the part of the Climate Bible that has the best reputation for rigor.

Unfortunately, that reputation begins to tarnish as soon as one examines the dates of the papers on which Working Group 1 bases its conclusions. In Chapter 2, six papers are cited that had not been published prior to January 2006. Nor had they been published prior to January 2007. Nevertheless, IPCC authors involved in that chapter decided, amongst themselves, that they were sound science.

The story's even worse in Chapter 11. In that instance, 17 papers cited by the IPCC didn't make their public debut until 2007. This means that conclusions in the hard science section of the Climate Bible are based on dozens of papers that were so recent they couldn't even have been described as hot-off-the-press. These papers remained entirely unknown to the larger scientific community at the time the IPCC chose to accept their findings.

Environmental activists frequently complain that the Climate Bible is too conservative because it provides no support for some of the more extreme predictions made by people such as Al Gore. But let us have perfect clarity on this point: An organization that is prepared to base its conclusions on dozens of as-yet-unpublished research papers is not conservative.

16 – THIS IS CALLED CHEATING

The IPCC says it conducts no research of its own. It says its merely surveys the already-available scientific literature on climate change and figures out what it all means.

But the fact that the IPCC cites *unpublished* papers tells us the playing field is skewed. People who know people at the IPCC have their yet-to-be-published work taken into account, but researchers without these sorts of connections are out of luck.

As usual, the more one probes the more irregularities one finds. According to an IPCC insider who answered the online questionnaire, scientists who want to include specific information in the Climate Bible aren't above manufacturing journal articles for that very purpose. In this person's words:

> Governments want the chapter to cover questions of current relevance for which there [is] often "grey literature" but little peer reviewed literature...An approach that has been used in such cases is that **lead authors try to have material published in peer reviewed journals while they are drafting the IPCC chapter so that the published or in press article can be cited** in the final draft of the IPCC chapter. [bold added, p. 68]

This is called cheating. And apparently it's an open secret that such things go on. Which means a lot of people know that the IPCC is not, in fact, conducting a neutral and objective assessment of already-available scientific literature. Instead, the system is being gamed at multiple levels and from multiple angles.

The above revelation sheds light on a curious discovery I made months prior to the questionnaire answers becoming public. It turns out that one particular issue of the journal *Climatic Change* was relied on to an implausible degree by the 2007 Climate Bible. When the IPCC cites 16 of 21 papers published between the covers of one particular issue of one particular scientific journal, it begins to look as though that issue was tailor-made for the convenience of the IPCC.

This, of course, would be a complete inversion of how things are supposed to work. Academic journals are supposed to be independent actors. They're supposed to receive random submissions of research papers that are then dispassionately examined by peer reviewers and published (or not) based on their individual merits.

But a problem surely arises when journals are run by IPCC insiders themselves. I've never seen anyone discuss this matter, but the implications here are profound. For example, until his death in 2010, *Climatic Change* was led by its founding editor, Stephen Schneider. [note 16-1] The fact that Schneider, a senior figure at the IPCC, was routinely deciding what would - and would not - make it into the same scientific literature the IPCC would later cite as evidence doesn't appear to have caused anyone concern.

But back to our implausibly helpful journal issue. Remember chairman Pachauri saying the cutoff date was *prior* to January 2006? And remember that the expert reviewers were given deadlines? In the two sections of the Climate Bible relevant to this discussion, those deadlines were June 2 and July 21, 2006.

So guess when this journal issue was published? Not until May 2007. Fifteen of those 16 papers weren't even *accepted* by the journal until mid-October 2006. [note 16-2]

Four separate chapters of the Climate Bible cited this May 2007 issue of *Climatic Change*. Chapter 11 relied on ten of these papers, including three co-authored by Jens Hessel-bjerg Christensen, one of the two leaders of Chapter 11. Later, this Danish climate modeler would serve as a guest editor of that very issue of *Climatic Change*.

To recap: An IPCC chapter relied on papers that hadn't even been accepted by a journal yet. One of the people in charge of that chapter was in a direct conflict-of-interest since he himself had authored some of them. The second conflict-of-interest occurred when this gentleman - as a journal guest editor - was subsequently responsible for adding these papers to the hallowed ranks of the peer-reviewed scientific literature.

There are lots of words for this - and none of them mean *independent*. This is a circular, incestuous process. Scientists make decisions as journal editors about what qualifies as peer-reviewed literature. They then cite the same papers they themselves played midwife to while serving as IPCC authors.

If you're starting to suspect that climate science is a small, insular world lacking any normal sense of propriety, welcome to the club. Genuine oversight, neutral parties - apparently these are foreign concepts.

The IPCC says its reports are based on already-published scientific literature. Yet in this case a group of IPCC authors appears to have favored a particular conclusion regardless of what the scientific literature actually said. The fact that necessary information hadn't yet been published posed no impediment. They simply wrote the IPCC chapter they desired and arranged for the necessary papers to be published after the fact.

Has anyone paid any price for behaving so outrageously? Given that Christensen was once again named a co-ordinating lead author for the edition of the Climate Bible currently underway, evidently not. [note 16-3]

Have I mentioned who took over the management of *Climatic Change* following Schneider's demise? It is now led by two co-editors. One of them is Michael Oppenheimer, the activist scientist discussed above. He's the gent who spent more than two decades employed by the Environmental Defense Fund.

At the same time that he's passing judgment on which research papers deserve to gain the 'peer-reviewed literature' stamp-of-approval Oppenheimer is also serving as an IPCC coordinating lead author.

Climatic Change's other editor is Gary Yohe. He, too, is currently an IPCC coordinating lead author. When considering the degree to which Yohe's judgment should be trusted readers may wish to consider the fact that his name appeared first under the web-published OpenLetterFromScientists discussed earlier.

That open letter praised the IPCC for its "excellent performance" and characterized criticism of this organization as "invented hyperbole."

17 – CROSS-EXAMINATION

Jason Johnston is a law professor at the University of Virginia. Prior to taking his current job he taught for 15 years at University of Pennsylvania, directing an environmental law program during much of that time.

In May 2010 Johnston uploaded an 82-page working paper titled *Global Warming Advocacy Science: a Cross Examination* to a scholarly depository. In that paper he performs a task lawyers undertake as a matter of course: he cross-examines an expert witness.

In this case, the expert witness is the IPCC. He points out that although trial lawyers often lack scientific training, this doesn't stop them from educating themselves about relevant issues and then asking tough questions in the courtroom.

In essence, Johnston performs a reality-check. Since many politicians regard IPCC conclusions as gospel - and have responded by initiating new taxes and intrusive regulations - Johnston makes an obvious point. One would think, he says, that before such measures are undertaken it would be useful to verify whether the IPCC reports really do represent "an unbiased and objective assessment." In his words:

such verification means comparing what the IPCC has to say about climate science with what one finds in the peer-reviewed climate science literature...

Much to Johnston's surprise, his own research discovered that, "on virtually every major issue in climate change science," IPCC reports "systematically conceal or minimize what appear to be fundamental scientific uncertainties."

According to Johnston, if one goes to the trouble of examining the full range of research conducted by "scientists at the very best universities" who are of "unimpeachable credibility," one discovers "a number of facts and findings that... are rarely if ever mentioned" in the Climate Bible.

For example, he devotes dozens of pages to explaining the shortcomings of climate models. According to these models, increased CO2 will cause the air near the surface of the planet to heat up. This effect is supposed to be especially pronounced in the atmosphere nearest the equator. Johnston says this second point gives us an opportunity to empirically test whether the models get it right.

Buried within the pages of the crucial attribution chapter of the 2007 Climate Bible, the IPCC acknowledges there's a problem. It admits (in none-too-clear language) that the extra heat isn't where the models say it should be. The real world isn't behaving the way the models predict it will.

Johnston observes that this leaves two possibilities: Either the real-world data is faulty "or something is wrong with the models." Guess which explanation the Climate Bible chooses? The authors of that chapter say the "probable explanation" is that real temperature data gathered in the real world is "contaminated by errors."

While the IPCC may be content with a *probable* explanation, the public surely deserves to be told that the climate models fail this important test. But as Johnston points out, this fact isn't even mentioned in the *Summary for Policymakers* document for that section of the Climate Bible. [note 17-1]

It's a similar story with the feedback controversy. As Warren Meyer - who blogs at Climate-Skeptic.com – explains, the climate catastrophe hypothesis actually has two parts. Part One is the straightforward greenhouse gas theory. It says that doubling the amount of CO_2 in the atmosphere (which, based on current trends, might occur by 2100) will cause some warming - approximately one degree Celsius. Few people consider an increase of one degree spread over a century anything to worry about.

The only way the planet ends up in climate catastrophe territory is if we accept the far more controversial Part Two - which *assumes* that the climate system is highly sensitive to small changes and that this one degree of warming will get amplified by two, three, or more hundred percent via something called positive feedback mechanisms. To quote Meyer:

Negative feedback means that when you disturb an object or system in some way, forces tend to counteract this disturbance. Positive feedback means that the forces at work tend to reinforce or magnify a disturbance.

Speaking as a mechanical engineer who has done academic work on feedbacks, Meyer says that "Almost every process you can think of in nature operates by negative feedback." Scientists typically assume negative feedbacks are at work, he says, unless someone proves otherwise. Except in climate science. Oddly, in that instance, "everyone assumes positive feedback is common."

Sounding astonished, law professor Johnston concludes that climate catastrophe is not an "*output* of climate analysis but an *input*" (his italics). Dramatic temperature increases are the result of an assumption, made by climate modelers, that CO_2's slight warming effect will get amplified. Yet "*no mention whatsoever* is made of the positive feedback" issue in the summary version of the IPCC report - the only version likely to be read by politicians and journalists (Johnston's italics). [note 17-2]

Incredible as it sounds, therefore, the only reason climate models tell us we are at risk of eco apocalypse is because the climate modelers believe our climate system behaves in a manner that is opposite to the way most natural systems behave. If the modelers had split themselves into two groups, half programming-in negative feedback and half programming-in positive feedback, the first group of models would predict nothing alarming.

Johnston discusses several scientific papers in reputable journals that suggest negative feedbacks are alive and well in the climate system. But he says that although these and other issues are being actively debated in the peer-reviewed scientific literature, one wouldn't know it from reading the Climate Bible.

Nowhere does the IPCC explain in a straightforward manner that some scientists think the climate models fail an important test - or that climate models have been pre-programmed to produce their scary conclusions.

In Johnston's profession there are legal *briefs* - and legal *memos*. A legal brief attempts to persuade people of a particular point-of-view.

Legal memos, on the other hand, objectively enumerate all the available and relevant facts - not just the pros, but the cons, as well. Not just the strengths, but the shortcomings, too. Being familiar with the pitfalls and weak links of their case enables lawyers to plan ahead for a variety of contingencies.

The IPCC is supposed to produce a report that is balanced and objective - like a legal memo. Armed with all the facts, legislators are then supposed to make informed decisions.

But Johnston's cross-examination concludes that the Climate Bible is actually the equivalent of a legal brief. Rather than providing all the facts, the IPCC has been leaving out important information. It has been tailoring its message.

18 – ENDANGERED: INDEPENDENT MINDS

Why would an organization that claims to be *scientific*, that says it is conducting a *scientific* assessment, produce a report that is skewed rather than objective?

There are many pieces to this jigsaw puzzle, but a large one is this: Strictly speaking, the IPCC is not - and has never been - a scientific body. Individual scientists do not belong to the IPCC. Nations do. That's why the IPCC tells us what country its authors represent and almost nothing else. International political considerations always come first at the IPCC. Scientific credibility comes second.

The IPCC has never asked the science academies of the world to identify the top experts in a number of fields - and then systematically recruited only those people. Instead, nominations are sought from governments.

This is a problem for a few reasons. In democratic countries, governments rise and fall. A US administration in which Al Gore was Vice President regarded climate issues differently than the next administration, in which Dick Cheney was VP.

This means that the political philosophy of whoever happens to be in office influences the IPCC author nomination process. Add in the fact that a country's environment ministry is usually the contact point for the IPCC and the problem becomes clearer. In many European countries, minority Green Party politicians are awarded the environment portfolio. Since it's unlikely that an environment department run by a Green Party politician would nominate the same list of experts as an environment department run by a Tory party politician, it becomes obvious that the selection of experts is colored by political - rather than scientific - considerations.

In countries that are not democracies, ruling cliques retain their position via secret police and military force. Staying on the good side of those in charge is vitally important. There are many places in this world where, if you say the wrong thing to the wrong person, the authorities break down your door in the middle of the night and drag you and your family off to prison.

Let us not be naive. How likely is it that world-class scientific experts will emerge from the chaos, corruption, and widespread poverty common in undemocratic countries? Even more to the point: Why would we suppose that those nominated for IPCC duty by unsavory governments are at liberty to form independent scientific conclusions? They would be courageous people, indeed, to adopt a position counter to the one decreed by their political bosses.

This is why the claim that the IPCC consists of scientists from 113 countries who've all independently come to the same conclusions is so misleading. All told, there are 195 nations in the world. According to the UN itself only a small fraction are developed economies. On this list are Australia, Austria, Belgium, Canada, Denmark, Finland, France, Germany, Greece, Italy, Luxembourg, Japan, New Zealand, Portugal, Spain, Sweden, the Netherlands, the UK and the US.

That makes a grand total of 19. Add in Russia, China, and Israel and the number of countries in a position to nurture first-class educational and research facilities is still less than two dozen.

The moment it was decided that the job of identifying the world's top scientific experts should be handed over to politicians from more than 100 countries (rather than to a handful of prestigious science academies) was the moment the IPCC ceased to be a scientific body.

Peel another layer from the onion, and things get even stickier. Earlier I mentioned that the NOAA - the US National Oceanic and Atmospheric Administration - devoted a page in one of its publications to celebrating its employees' involvement with the IPCC. According to that page "more than 120 NOAA scientists contributed" to the 2007 Climate Bible.

In itself, that is a startling number. A single US government organization had 120 employees taking part in IPCC activities. Is every last one of them really a world-class expert?

But there's an even more important question: Were these people truly free to come to their own, independent conclusions as IPCC authors? Were they provided with written assurance that, should their scientific conscience lead them in a direction at odds with the organization that pays their salary, they were at liberty to follow their conscience?

The IPCC is supposed to objectively evaluate the scientific literature regarding climate change. But if 120 of the IPCC's personnel are from the NOAA, and if the NOAA has already decided that human activity is causing climate change, how neutral can these people be expected to be?

The NOAA has spent a ton of money on climate models that have, in turn, been used by the IPCC to make its arguments. The NOAA is therefore unlikely to be a workplace where people will receive promotions for questioning the climate change party line.

In this regard, an anecdote from *The Climate Caper*, a book by an Australian atmospheric scientist, is illuminating:

> In the early nineties I was involved in setting up an Antarctic research centre...to examine the role of Antarctica and the Southern Ocean in global climate. I made the error at the time of mentioning in a media interview - reported extensively in 'The Australian' on a slow Easter Sunday - that there were still lots of doubts about the disaster potential of global warming. Suffice it to say that within a couple of days it was made very clear to me from the highest levels of [Australia's premier scientific body - CSIRO] that, should I make such public comments again, then it would pull out of the

process of forming the new Centre...[which] would have killed the whole thing dead...

The author, Garth Paltridge, goes on to say that at the time he gave his interview, the Commonwealth Scientific and Industrial Research Organization (CSIRO) was attempting to secure additional funding from the Australian government. Now that he is retired and able to speak freely, Paltridge points out that most science research money is provided by governments. It then gets distributed via a handful of funding agencies run by administrators.

Science administrators are always eager to expand their budgets. Over the past 20 years they've learned that sounding climate alarm bells is an effective way to secure additional resources. They understand perfectly that it's in their interest to ride the climate wave.

This means that scientists who raise uncomfortable questions - or who voice doubts to journalists - risk offending those in charge of the purse strings. Like Paltridge, they discover that their own funding may evaporate if they don't keep their mouths shut.

The inevitable result, says Paltridge, is that political leaders seeking straight answers now have "nowhere to turn for a second opinion." Scientific *institutions* have adopted a point-of-view on climate change because that point-of-view serves these institutions' financial interests.

This is a grim conclusion, since it implies that even if science bodies were nominating experts to work on the Climate Bible, the situation might not be significantly better. No one, it seems, now considers it their role to safeguard the integrity of science itself.

Toward the end of his book, Paltridge discusses the social psychology of the climate science world. He paints a picture in which too many people are graduating with research science credentials than can reasonably be employed in their fields. It's therefore not uncommon for bright, highly trained people to find themselves in a rut, doing unsatisfying work that is unlikely to win them much notice.

And then along comes the IPCC. It offers them a sense of purpose, an opportunity to be a hero, a chance to save the world. It invites them to meetings in exotic locales. It links their name to a Nobel prize. It gives the media a reason to treat them like celebrities.

Many people would find all of this intoxicating. Some of them, surely, might be tempted to swallow their personal misgivings, to tell themselves that all those other smart people must be right about the climate change threat even if they themselves aren't entirely persuaded. [note 18-1]

19 – THE INTERNATIONAL POLITICAL STAGE

Declaring that the IPCC is a political body rather than a scientific one is easy. It takes no effort to make such a statement. In the blogosphere, people say this all the time. But since we often see what we expect to see, that hardly settles the matter. The real question is whether this is a reasonable conclusion after a careful, fair-minded examination of the situation.

Two years of research later it has become clear to me that the IPCC is, indeed, all about politics. Once you know what to look for the evidence is pretty much out in the open - and it comes from IPCC insiders themselves.

Scientific bodies, the media, bureaucrats, politicians - all of these have told us the IPCC's purpose is to summarize what we know about climate change. Indeed, in the first chapter of this book I, too, made that statement. I said the IPCC's job is *to survey the scientific literature regarding climate change, to decide what it all means, and to write an ongoing series of reports.*

Like most people, I assumed such reports are needed so that governments can make sound decisions. Political leaders around the world do, indeed, point to IPCC documents as the reason they believe certain things and are pursuing certain policies. Everyone from the US Environmental Protection Agency to the UK Advertising Standards Authority considers IPCC reports authoritative.

But it was only after I read the nearly 700 pages of answers from the online questionnaire, where actual IPCC participants say the same thing again and again in different ways, that a new piece of the puzzle fell into place. What those participants are well aware of, but what is rarely pointed out to the public, is that the Climate Bible plays a specific role on the international stage.

As far as the United Nations is concerned, without the Climate Bible there could be no climate talks. In order for climate negotiations to get anywhere, everyone first needs to be on the same page. If one country reported that its glaciers are advancing and another said the opposite, the process would be sidetracked by innumerable disputes over what's really going on.

The Climate Bible, therefore, represents a common understanding. It is a *political* document that nails down a shared view of climate-related matters among *political* leaders of various countries. Its primary purpose is to enable certain kinds of international *political* discussions to take place.

Since 1992, the UN has sponsored an ongoing series of meetings aimed at curbing the world's greenhouse gas emissions. On a regular basis representatives of UN countries gather in places such as Rio, Bali, and Cancun to conduct these discussions.

Calling the UN climate talks a circus sounds unkind, but it's actually an apt description. Thousands of those who attend these multi-day events are professional activists. They're employed by groups such as Greenpeace, the WWF, Friends of the Earth, the David Suzuki Foundation, and so forth. These groups are granted official observer status by the UN. Their goal, it appears, is to create the impression that there's widespread public support for drastic emissions cuts.

But activists are not elected by - or accountable to - anyone. They claim to speak for 'civil society' but are in fact advancing a political philosophy decidedly to the left of center. If a large segment of the public supported that philosophy the Green Party would be a serious political force. The fact that it remains a minority player in most affluent countries tells us its vision isn't one the average person finds appealing.

The official delegations from various nations are usually dominated by environment ministry bureaucrats. Some of these people spend a good part of their lives on planes, flying to one UN-sponsored event after another. Nice work if you can get it, but such people have no incentive to conclude that the entire process is an expensive, unproductive waste of time.

During climate negotiations, activists stage publicity stunts intended to embarrass government officials into making ill-considered commitments. Since those government officials are already predisposed to think urgent action is necessary, this is a problem. Lots of folks want to defend Mother Nature, but no one seems to be speaking for ordinary people.

It's all very well to be concerned about CO_2 emissions. But life is about tradeoffs. What can reasonably be accomplished, and what is a reasonable price to pay? Everything we do requires energy - refrigerating our food, cooking our meals, heating our homes and schools, powering our hospitals, traveling to our workplaces, and ferrying our elderly relatives to their medical appointments. At this moment in history the cheapest, most reliable energy comes from fossil fuels - primarily coal, oil, and gas. All of these emit some amount of CO_2.

The only way, in the short term, to drastically reduce CO_2 emissions would be for governments to sharply increase the cost of energy. If the price of electricity were to quadruple overnight many factories would shut down because they couldn't afford to pay their hydro bill. Those factories assemble computers and smoke detectors. They preserve food under sanitary conditions. They manufacture medicine and eyeglasses. They employ your neighbour and your sister-in-law.

If the price of gasoline were to quadruple, trucking companies would lay off most of their drivers and perishable goods would rot in warehouses rather than reaching customers. Nurses who visit patients at home could no longer afford to fill up their gas tanks, and getting your child to swimming lessons would be too costly.

Activists say *drastic* measures are called for. But if you look closely at the numbers and timelines they toss around, it's unlikely their targets could be reached without throwing half the population out-of-work.

Most of us don't consider plunging the world into misery an acceptable solution to environmental concerns. Society may not have produced as much CO2 back in the 1930s, but that doesn't change the fact that the Great Depression was a tragic, soul-destroying time.

There's also another problem. An integral component of the climate talks involves rich countries helping poorer ones adapt to climate change by giving them money and technology. In itself this may be an admirable thing. But the plan is for rich countries to transfer vast amounts of money into a fund that the UN will administer. In other words, giving the UN control over a mountain of new cash is one of the goals of a climate treaty.

It isn't hard to see why UN bureaucrats think this is a great idea, but what about the views of ordinary working people who pay the taxes that will eventually end up in this UN bank account? When's the last time they were asked how they felt about this arrangement - or whether they preferred an alternative one? When's the last time the pros and cons were clearly explained to them?

For that matter, when have we ever had a serious discussion about how *unaccountable* the UN actually is? New York city, which hosts the UN's headquarters, can't even get UN personnel to pay their parking tickets. Over a recent five-year period they accumulated 150,000 unpaid tickets amounting to $18 million in fines.

It turns out that UN personnel from countries in which corruption is rampant demonstrate the most contempt for parking laws and are the least likely to pay their tickets. In other words, many UN officials don't come from countries that encourage them to behave in a circumspect manner. These people don't believe they are answerable for their transgressions, or that the rules even apply to them. Yet these are some of the people who'd help decide the fate of billions of climate-related dollars.

To get an idea of what the UN's climate appropriations committee might look like, we need look no further than the makeup of something called the IPCC bureau. This is its senior leadership, the people responsible for coordinating the overall process. At the moment, this 31-member bureau includes *two* members from Sudan - a basket case of a country. Since seizing power in a military coup, the president of Sudan has been accused of orchestrating war crimes in Darfur. According to international observers, the 2010 Sudanese election was rigged. Life expectancy there is 55 years.

Countries such as Iran, Saudi Arabia, China, Cuba, and Malaysia also have seats on the IPCC bureau. In 2009 Iranian authorities horrified the world by attacking peaceful protesters. Observers from Amnesty International have not been allowed into Cuba since 1990. In Malaysia the government suspends newspapers and arrests bloggers.

The Maldives, a tiny island nation with a population of less than half a million, also has a seat on the IPCC bureau. In that country people (usually women) are publicly flogged for engaging in extra-marital sex. Madagascar, too, has IPCC bureau representation. In early 2009 its elected president was deposed by a military coup. The rule of law is so elastic in that nation that, following the coup, its high court declared the new military ruler legitimate - despite the fact that he was only 34 years old and Madagascar law said presidents must be at least 40.

To sum up, therefore, the IPCC is a child of the United Nations. The UN includes a number of unsavory countries run by violent, unaccountable governments. We can avert our eyes and refuse to think about what this means. Or we can confront the unpleasant fact that IPCC reports are an essential link in a chain. That chain leads to taxpayers like you and me funding UN programs where nations such as these wield influence.

20 – THE CART BEFORE THE HORSE

At an event celebrating the IPCC's 20th anniversary, its chairman gave a speech in which he publicly acknowledged that the IPCC's primary purpose is not to help governments make wise climate change decisions. Rather, in his words:

> The UNFCCC is our main customer, if I could label them as such, and our interaction with them enriches the relevance of our work...

UNFCCC stands for the United Nations Framework Convention on Climate Change. This international treaty was launched in 1992 at the Earth Summit held in Rio de Janeiro. When the chairman of the IPCC says his organization's main purpose is to assist a UN body that administers a *political* agreement between nations - what he's really telling us is that there's no conceivable way the Climate Bible can be an objective scientific document.

What's happened here is that the cart was put before the horse. The UN didn't wait around for climate science to mature. Rather, 19 years ago, bigwigs at the UN had already accused, tried, and convicted greenhouse gases. They'd already decided that human-generated emissions were dangerous.

Back in 1992, 154 nations endorsed this premature conclusion when they became signatories to the UNFCCC. (Some would later agree to reduce their CO2 emissions when they signed on to the Kyoto Protocol, which is a component of the UNFCCC process.) [note 20-1]

One must remember that the UN is the mother of all bureaucracies. Bureaucrats always try to expand their man-date, their funding, and their prestige. The idea that human-generated emissions were a global environmental problem - and that this problem could be solved via a grand global treaty - was no doubt appealing to UN personnel. It placed them at the center of the action.

Step one was the *political* decision that a greenhouse gas treaty was a worthy and achievable goal. Step two was the recognition that before such a treaty could be negotiated, certain documents - representing a common understanding - were required. Step three involved enlisting scientists to help produce such documents.

Please note that the UN could have erected a firewall between the IPCC's scientific activities and the UNFCCC's political machinations - but it chose not to. Being circumspect about such matters is so alien a concept that Rajendra Pachauri, above, says the IPCC's close connection to the UNFCCC *enriches* his organization.

It is abundantly clear, therefore, that the IPCC doesn't write scientific reports for their own sake. Those scientists are there for a purpose. That purpose is to produce material useful to the UNFCCC.

The UNFCCC has spent the past 20 years demanding that we all curb our emissions. In 2007 its director, Yvo de Boer, declared that failing to do so would be "nothing less than criminally irresponsible."

This is a situation in which political operators (UN bureaucrats) pursuing a political goal (a greenhouse gas treaty) have recruited scientists to help them achieve their objective.

There might not be anything wrong with that if everyone was upfront and honest about these facts. Instead, we're constantly told that *science says* we have to do something about emissions. But that isn't the order in which things actually happened.

The first, shortest, and most quickly written edition of the Climate Bible appeared in 1990. Its findings were tentative. Yet by June 1992, aided by environmental activists, the UN had successfully convinced a majority of the world's governments to sign a framework document that declared greenhouse gases to be arch villains.

The fourth edition of the Climate Bible, which contains the strongest (yet still speculative and qualified) language, appeared 15 years *later*.

21 – WHAT'S A NICE SCIENTIST LIKE YOU DOING IN A PLACE LIKE THIS?

When I began reading the responses that IPCC insiders provided to the online questionnaire, I was struck by how many times the term *buy-in* appears. According to one coordinating lead author: "International action on climate change needs universal government 'buy-in' on the state of knowledge. The purpose of the IPCC is to provide the mechanism for this..."

Someone else says: "Government buy-in is the main raison d'etre of the IPCC."

Remarks such as these appear frequently in response to a question that asked people for their views on the adoption of the Climate Bible at large IPCC meetings (often called plenaries). At these meetings scientists are out-numbered by politicians, environmental bureaucrats, and diplomats.

It's worth pointing out that the 2007 edition of the Climate Bible is 3,000 pages long. The average politician or journalist will never read more than a fraction of that. The IPCC therefore prepares an executive summary for each of the three smaller reports that comprise the full Climate Bible *enchilada*.

Called a *Summary for Policymakers*, these documents are a few dozen pages in length. Now here's the punch line: Scientists only *draft* these documents. The final wording is argued over, line-by-line, at those large IPCC meetings that drag on for days.

You heard that right: the only IPCC documents likely to be read by outsiders aren't scientific statements at all. Before the public is permitted to see them, *Summary for Policymakers* documents are subject to a process of political cleansing.

Were these meetings televised, most people would need witness only one of them before they lost any remaining illusions about the IPCC being a science-driven organization that produces science-based reports. But these meetings take place behind closed doors. Representatives from activist organizations are permitted to observe the proceeding - but journalists are barred. (Remember Pachauri's claim that "Whatever we do is available for scrutiny at every stage"? Not quite.) [note 21-1]

IPCC insiders who answered the online questionnaire expressed strong opinions about these meetings. Below are comments from three people:

- I suspect that...anyone who has not been involved in this process would scarcely believe how this meeting is managed; the expense, the length of the sessions, and the apparent pickiness of some of the discussion would strike many as a very poor way to conduct international business. (p. 114)
- this was an agonizing, frustrating process, as every sentence had to be wordsmithed on a screen in front of representatives of more than 100 governments, falling farther and farther beyond a realistic schedule by the hour. In Brussels in 2007, the process ran all night on the two final days. (p. 334)
- In my experience the summary for policy makers tends to be more of a political process than one of scientific précis. (p. 278)

While some who answered the questionnaire were adamant that the scientific content of these summaries survived these meetings intact, others took the opposite view. No doubt different meetings have had different dynamics. The essential point would seem to be: If nothing truly significant is going on at these meetings, why bother with them at all? Why doesn't the IPCC just publish the summaries written by the scientists themselves?

Given that numerous IPCC insiders complained loudly about what goes on at these plenaries, why aren't scientists refusing to take part in this process? Don't they understand that their participation permits the IPCC to dress up a profoundly political endeavor in scientific clothing?

That so many scientists continue to volunteer their time, for years at a stretch, to the IPCC leads to a troubling conclusion. Here are a few more verbatim quotes from the questionnaire answers. Remember, these are scientists talking:

- There are obvious concerns with regard to line by line approval of the summary of a scientific document by government representatives. However, on the other hand the key reason for IPCC's influence has been engagement and buy in by the governments. I am much less concerned, compared to others, about this aspect of the IPCC process. (p. 365)
- The IPCC is a strange hybrid. Therefore necessarily messy. But also necessary to get buy in. (p. 413)
- One could imagine a scientist-controlled Panel...but it is not going to happen. The great advantage of the current government-controlled IPCC is that the governments cannot easily reject the IPCC findings after the fact...The price paid for this government buy-in can be steep, but that is just a fact of life. (pp. 85-86)

In each case, we see individuals making judgment calls. They know science isn't in the driver's seat at the IPCC. But each of them, after assessing the situation, rationalizes their own involvement. Each has his or her own reasons for continuing to be a cog in the UN climate treaty machine.

What the world needs to understand is that these reasons have nothing to do with science.

According to another individual, "The process is difficult, but I see that it serves its purpose of binding governments to the scientific facts" (p. 112). I think this person has things exactly backward. The *Summary for Policymakers* documents are similar to diplomatic treaties. When every word is carefully negotiated we can be sure that any scientific facts that happen to survive are there for one purpose only: to promote a handful of political agendas.

Governments aren't recognizing the supremacy of scientific facts. Rather, scientists are being outmaneuvered and outclassed. While those who work on IPCC reports may be accomplished in their own field, there is no reason to believe they are any match for people with decades of experience in international political intrigue.

One day the IPCC may come to be seen as a textbook case of how badly things can go wrong when political amateurs are recruited and manipulated by UN-grade political operatives.

22 – SCIENCE HAS (NOT) SPOKEN

The answers to the online questionnaire make one thing apparent: Many participating scientists are fully aware that the IPCC is controlled by politicians and that its reports serve a larger political purpose.

Which is why it's doubly distressing that, out here in the real world, people point to IPCC reports and claim that *science has spoken*. No, a highly politicized body - cloaking itself in the prestige and authority of science - has spoken.

In November 2007, Ban Ki-moon, the Secretary General of the United Nations, addressed an IPCC meeting. The occasion was the public release of the final segment of the 2007 Climate Bible - the summary of all summaries called the *Synthesis Report*. "Today," he declared, "the world's scientists have spoken, clearly and with one voice."

This is a gross distortion. According to a 2008 chart produced by the American Association for the Advancement of Science there are 5.8 *million* science and engineering researchers worldwide. No more than four *thousand* souls have ever been involved with the IPCC at any given time. In no sense whatsoever can the small minority of people connected to the IPCC be considered *the world's scientists*.

As I've mentioned, the 2007 Climate Bible is 3,000 pages long. In most cases, individuals were involved with only one or two chapters out of a total of 44. Most of them would freely admit they lack the relevant expertise to make judgments about many other sections of the report. Indeed, it would be surprising if even 10% of IPCC-affiliated scientists have even read all 3,000 pages.

Every IPCC scientist does not agree with every word on every page of this mammoth report. No single chapter - not even a single statement - has ever been endorsed by all the scientists affiliated with the IPCC. To suggest that these scientists are speaking *with one voice* is therefore misleading in the extreme.

But the head of the UN isn't the only one promoting a distorted view of reality. Three days after he delivered his address the *New York Times* ran an editorial titled *The Scientists Speak* in which it urged every member of Congress to read the IPCC's summary of summaries. The editorial said not one word about the fact that this document wasn't the unadorned words of scientific experts, but what's left over after five days of high-level message massaging at an IPCC plenary.

This is a good example of how the media, rather than keeping the IPCC honest, has encouraged its bad behavior. First the IPCC starts with a document drafted by scientists. Next politicians, bureaucrats, and diplomats re-write this document in secret. Rather than telling their readers, viewers, and listeners that this is a highly unusual process at tremendous risk of political manipulation, media outlets are totally cool with this - to the extent that they don't even think these facts are worth mentioning.

In late 2010 Australia's *Sydney Morning Herald* published the headline: *Science has spoken on climate change, it's now up to politicians.* One would never know, from reading the text beneath, that politicians have long exercised authority over what words, precisely, 'science' has been allowed to utter.

That scientific integrity takes a back seat at the IPCC has been confirmed explicitly by its chairman. When asked, during a 2007 interview, why the summary of the first section of the Climate Bible had been released before the full text was available, Rajendra Pachauri said there was a perfectly logical explanation.

(This, by the way, is standard IPCC practice. A cynic might describe it as one of the ways in which the IPCC manipulates media coverage. At the time that reporters are writing their main news story they have no way of independently verifying that the summary provided by the IPCC is an accurate reflection of the more lengthy document. They simply have to trust that this is the case. Later, when the full report is finally released, reporters have moved on and the matter is no longer newsworthy.)

Pachauri explained that the draft version of the summary, written by IPCC scientists, had undergone some changes during the plenary. In his opinion, these changes were not significant. (Once again, this oh-so-transparent organization expects us to simply take its word for it. Since journalists weren't allowed to observe this process, they can't come to their own conclusions.) Nevertheless, said Pachauri, "we necessarily have to ensure that the underlying report conforms to the refinements."

So there we have it - straight from the horse's mouth. The chairman of the IPCC admits that, after the politicians have had their say, the IPCC goes back to the original Climate Bible chapters written by its various groups of authors. It matters not that the IPCC has proclaimed these authors the world's top experts. What they've written must give ground.

According to the chairman himself, the IPCC tweaks their words *so that the underlying scientific sections accord with the version of reality that was hammered out by the politicians.*

Once one understands that this is how things are done, reading the newspaper can become an exercise in self-restraint. An unending chorus of activists, journalists, and politicians continue to promote the myth that, via the IPCC, *science has spoken.*

The implication is that we all now have a moral imperative to fall into line. No doubts are allowed. No debate is permitted. In late 2009, just prior to the UNFCCC climate talks in Copenhagen, a particularly ugly piece of journalism appeared in a UK newspaper. It quoted that country's Prime Minister, Gordon Brown, as follows:

"With only days to go before Copenhagen we mustn't be distracted by the behind-the-times, anti-science, flat-earth climate sceptics," Brown told the *Guardian*. "We know the science. We know what we must do."

Next, the UK's environment secretary, Ed Miliband, described climate skeptics as "saboteurs." He continued:

The sceptics are playing politics with science in a dangerous and deceitful manner...The evidence is clear and the time we have to act is short.

We know the science. Except that that science has been interfered with by politicians. *Skeptics are playing politics.* Since the IPCC is itself part of an elaborate political machine, that's rich.

A month earlier and thousands of miles away the Australian Prime Minister, Kevin Rudd, had delivered a speech in which he'd pointed to the 2007 IPCC report to make his case. People who question the Climate Bible's findings are cowardly and intellectually dishonest, he said. The idea that there's any real debate about climate change is, in his words:

...a political attempt to subvert what is now a long-standing scientific consensus, an attempt to twist the agreed science in the direction of a **predetermined political agenda**... [bold added] [note 22-1]

Honestly. The IPCC was established by politicians, its experts are selected by politicians, and its conclusions are negotiated by politicians. A predetermined political agenda has been part of the landscape for the past 20 years.

For Rudd, Miliband, Brown - or anyone else - to whine that people who disagree with the IPCC are motivated by *politics* is the equivalent of someone who has lived by the sword complaining that they might die by it.

23 – SCIENCE IS NOT A TYRANT

In December 2007 Sweden's environment minister, Andreas Carlgren, gave a speech at a UNFCCC meeting in Bali. It contained these embarrassing claims:

> Science has given crystal clear confirmation of what is required of us to avoid a dramatic threat to our earth's climate...Science urges us that we therefore need to limit global warming to 2 degrees...By 2050 the emissions need to be reduced by at least 50 to 85 percent. This is what IPCC tells us.

In fact, almost nothing about climate science can be characterized as 'crystal clear.' If matters really were that straightforward a report by an advisory council prepared for Carlgren's own ministry and published only four days after his Bali speech, would not have concluded something rather different:

> It is worth noting that the IPCC **has not taken a position** on the level at which temperature rise is or may be deemed to be harmful. [bold added] [note 23-1]

According to Carlgren, with the IPCC serving as its spokesperson, science has pointed to a thermometer and told us precisely what amount of warming will be dangerous. But other people - including the authors of a report favorable to the IPCC - insist that no such thing has occurred. If this is what clarity looks like, heaven save us from confusion.

We all need to understand that climate science involves a great deal of uncertainty. Our knowledge is sparse, at best. Since this planet is 4.5 *billion* years old, and since humans have been around for only about 250,000 years - we're late-comers to the party. Even worse, we only began recording temperatures on a somewhat global scale 150 years ago.

When you think about it, it isn't terribly plausible that scientists relying on such meager data can know for certain that current temperature fluctuations aren't part of a multi-hundred (or multi-thousand) year natural cycle.

Activists and journalists love to play the 'science says' game. But the proper role of a scientist is to collect and interpret data. Even in cases in which everyone has full confidence in the accuracy of that data, how we should *respond* to it is a separate discussion.

Imagine that city officials knock on my door one day and tell me that an unusual ground fissure has formed at the far end of my street. I'm told the city has a plan for dealing with the situation, but if things don't work out, there's a chance the fissure could expand and my house could eventually be swallowed up.

In such an instance I have a range of choices, each with its own pluses and minuses:

- I can try to sell my house and move immediately - before all my neighbors decide to do the same thing.
- After conducting some research, I can conclude that the city's approach to dealing with the problem has been successful on other occasions, so there's little to worry about.
- My neighbors and I can pool our resources and hire an expert to provide us with a second opinion.

- I can decide that, if the fissure spreads beyond a certain point, that's when I'll put a 'For Sale' sign on my front lawn.

The fissure is a scientific fact. But there's no hand-lettered sign reaching out from its depths with 'crystal clear confirmation' about how we should respond to it. Different people on my street will choose to do different things - depending on how much they like their current home, what level of faith they have in city officials, whether or not this is a good time to be selling property, whether their children are having nightmares, and so forth.

In other words, even if it's true that the modest warming caused by human-generated CO2 will get amplified by positive feedbacks in the atmosphere (rather than dampened by negative ones), how individuals, communities, and nations should respond is up for debate:

- Should we place our faith in new technologies, trusting that human ingenuity will find a way to neutralize excess carbon dioxide before global warming becomes acute?
- Should we focus the bulk of our attention on shoring up seawalls - and on ensuring that adequate water supplies are available to those most at risk of drought?
- Should we triple-check the world's temperature records, just to make sure that the few tenths of a degree change that has everyone in a tizzy aren't, in fact, the result of errors?
- Should we trust that future generations will be smart, well-equipped human beings capable of taking care of themselves?
- Or should we declare that the **one and only acceptable solution** is drastic worldwide emissions reductions starting now?

When politicians such as the Swedish environment minister insist that 'science says' that more than half of our emissions must cease within a few decades, they've decided to skip the debate altogether. They haven't placed a range of scenarios before the public. They haven't invited us to discuss the pluses and minuses (*aka* the tradeoffs) of competing approaches.

Instead, they've decided that only one response will do.

There is nothing democratic about this. This is an example of a small group of people imposing their own opinions on everyone else. These people are implying that science is a tyrant, that ground fissures come with an instruction manual identifying the one acceptable way to respond to them.

Nice try. But if Al Gore is right and we're experiencing a *planetary emergency* we need all the brainpower and all the debate we can get. If Ban Ki-moon is correct about climate change being the *defining challenge of our age* the inhabitants of this planet are entitled to know what our full range of choices really are.

Politicians frequently say that *science demands* emissions reductions. Journalists tell us that "*science says* reductions of at least 25 to 40 percent are necessary."

The next time you hear such confident proclamations remind yourself that those who play 'science says' are denying the wider community a voice.

There is, of course, a rather obvious reason why IPCC personnel believe emissions reduction is the answer. For a long time I was puzzled by the fact that the climate change discussion is a package deal. Not only are we told there's a problem, we're being sold one particular solution. That didn't feel right.

Now, it all makes sense. The IPCC's chairman, remember, has declared that his organization's "main customer" isn't ordinary people or even the governments of the world. The IPCC's purpose is - ding, ding, ding - to support the UNF-CCC climate talks.

Since the UNFCCC is an emissions treaty, of course large numbers of people affiliated with the IPCC think emissions reduction is the best response. Duh.

24 – A SOLUTION IN SEARCH OF A PROBLEM

In the land of the IPCC, words don't mean the same thing they do elsewhere. On the IPCC's own website, its description of itself ends with the claim that this organization is "policy-neutral, never policy-prescriptive." This is another way of saying that the IPCC is supposed to stick to the science and let other people figure out humanity's responses.

But as we've seen, the IPCC's *main purpose* is to make UNFCCC negotiations possible. Since international emissions treaties are, in fact, a government policy it makes no sense to say the IPCC is policy-neutral.

Moreover, in speeches and interviews the personnel associated with this *never-policy-prescriptive* body have long advocated specific measures. Rather than setting a good example in this regard, some of the worst offenders have been top IPCC officials.

The problem here is twofold. Every time they advocate a particular response to climate change, IPCC personnel are overstepping their mandate. But it also turns out that many of these responses are lifted straight from the playbook of hardcore environmentalists.

A certain type of person has long believed that humanity has fouled its nest and that our survival is imperiled. Never let it be said that environmentalists don't believe in recycling. They've been pushing this same analysis for decades. But here's the important point: No matter what they said the problem of the moment was - over-population, ozone depletion, acid rain, global warming - environmentalists have long advocated the same basket of solutions.

These solutions amount to humanity forsaking industrialized society and a good measure of individual freedom. Apparently the answer is a return to Eden - to a slower, greener, more 'natural' pace of life that embraces traditional values rather than mindless consumerism.

Nothing prevents individuals from making those kinds of lifestyle choices for themselves. But that's not good enough. Citing the authority of scientific experts, hardcore environmentalists have long yearned to impose their vision on everyone else.

Four decades ago, in 1970, the first issue of *The Ecologist* magazine appeared in the UK. Its two-page editorial argued that when humans began farming, mining, and congregating in cities we stopped being part of the balanced natural world and instead became ecological *parasites*. Written by the magazine's founder, Edward Goldsmith, the editorial compared humanity to an *infection* and a *disease* that "is still spreading."

Known as the 'Godfather of Green,' Goldsmith - who died in 2009 - was no easy-going hippie. Rather, his writings suggest a harsh, dogmatic patriarch who thought it was his business to micromanage the lives of other people.

In 1970, Goldsmith was convinced that the 'population explosion' threatened us with extinction. He said we risked turning the Earth "into a lifeless waste," and declared that the "planet's stock of minerals and fossil fuels...is already sadly depleted" and would soon be exhausted. Sounding very much like an old fogey, he also denounced technology - warning that it would "collapse like a house of cards."

According to Goldsmith, humans no longer "fulfil their *correct* ecological functions" and our population has grown too rapidly for society to maintain its "*correct* structure" (the italics here, and below, are mine). Nor can he be accused of being a fan of democracy - a system in which authority flows from ordinary people to their elected representatives and in which those representatives keep their jobs only so long as a majority of people are prepared to tolerate their policies.

In the world envisioned by Goldsmith, government shouldn't answer to the people. Instead it should play the role of *schoolmaster* to "an ever more demanding and self-indulgent electorate."

According to Goldsmith, the purpose of education isn't to teach people how to think for themselves but to brainwash them into paying less attention to "their standard of living" so they can "fulfil their *correct* functions as members of their families, communities and eco-system." People shouldn't live wherever they choose, but in self-contained communities that eliminate the environmental harm associated with commuting to work or traveling abroad.

The Godfather of Green, in other words, belonged to a long line of authoritarian thinkers. Such people come from both the left and the right of the political spectrum - as well as from a variety of religious traditions. Goldsmith wasn't comfortable with individuals making their own choices about their own private lives. Rather, he believed a group of self-appointed experts/guardians/priests should be in charge.

Such an attitude should send shivers down the spine of anyone who, for example, thinks women have a right to control their own bodies. According to Goldsmith, everything would potentially need to be meddled with. In his words: "to control population we may have to interfere with 'personal liberty'..."

Two years later *The Ecologist* devoted an entire issue to a document titled *A Blueprint for Survival*. Later published as a book, by 1978 it had sold half a million copies and had been translated into 16 languages.

The preface declared that, if trends were *allowed to persist*, they'd lead to "irreversible disruption of the life-support systems on this planet." Therefore "a new philosophy of life" was required:

> our *Blueprint for Survival* heralds the formation of the **Movement for Survival** and, it is hoped, the dawn of a new age in which Man will learn to live with the rest of Nature rather than against it. [bold in the original]

A new philosophy of life. The dawn of a new age. Nothing so modest as cleaning up a few waterways and behaving more responsibly was being proposed.

As is the case today, the media fell for it. According to the London *Sunday Times*, the *Blueprint* was "Nightmarishly convincing...after reading it nothing seems quite the same any more." [note 24-1]

The language used in that 40-year-old book is almost identical to what we hear today. According to the first sentence of the introduction, our industrial way of life is not *sustainable*. The next page talks about the *urgent and radical measures* that must be taken. A few pages later, humanity is declared to be dumber than cows:

> Industrial man in the world today is like a bull in a china shop, with the single difference that a bull with half the information about the properties of china as we have about those of ecosystems would probably try and adapt its behaviour to its environment rather than the reverse. By contrast, *Homo sapiens industrialis* is determined that the china shop should adapt to him, and has therefore set himself the goal of reducing it to rubble in the shortest possible time. [italics in the original]

Please note this noxious view of humanity: while cows would *probably* start to take note of their surroundings, we delight in destroying our environment as quickly as possible - and for no apparent purpose.

What does all of this have to do with the IPCC? One of the reasons the *Blueprint* was taken so seriously 40 years ago is because it was endorsed "by 34 distinguished biologists, ecologists, doctors and economists." At the beginning of that book - together with a list of their degrees and affiliations - these people said they fully supported "the analysis of the problems we face today and the solutions proposed."

Four decades ago, therefore, men of science were already lending their support to activist, alarmist campaigns led by people who view the rest of us as dim-witted children in need of a stern schoolmaster.

The IPCC, therefore, represents the continuation of a tradition. Even though their professional expertise is limited to a narrow field, long before the IPCC was established some scientists believed they possessed special insight into much broader *political* questions.

I'm sure it's gratifying to take part in exercises such as this - to receive a VIP pass to closed-door meetings in which important discussions take place. But it all amounts to scientists playing house. Complex, deeply rooted human behaviors cannot be swept aside by the sheer brainpower of people who happen to hold a PhD in a scientific specialty.

There is no reason to believe that the average chemist has any more insight into what the future holds - or how society could successfully be reshaped - than does the average CEO. In both cases, their *opinions* are just that.

25 – PACHAURI'S CAUSE

In 2008, IPCC chairman Rajendra Pachauri declared in a speech: "We in the IPCC do not prescribe any specific action, but action is a must."

Gee, it must have been some other Rajendra Pachauri who, during an interview with Yale University's *Environment 360* magazine a few months prior, made verbatim remarks such as these:

- a price on carbon is absolutely essential.
- we need to bring down emissions very rapidly.

This interview is yet another demonstration of the kid gloves with which the IPCC has been treated by the media. This wasn't a situation in which the head of one of the world's most influential bodies was carefully evaluated by the editor and senior editor of an important environmental publication. Rather, Pachauri received rock star treatment. He was told by those interviewing him: "welcome back to New Haven. We are absolutely delighted and *honored* to have you as *our guest*" (my italics).

During that interview, Pachauri was repeatedly invited to talk about things that have nothing to do with science. He was asked for his reaction to a recent statement by the US president. He was asked what rich countries should do to help poor ones. He was invited to imagine he had been granted "benign dictatorial powers" and queried as to what concrete steps he would take immediately.

Repeatedly, Pachauri obliged. The leader of what is supposed to be a policy-neutral body participated in an extended policy discussion.

Pachauri could have explained that it would be inappropriate for him to express an opinion on such matters. He could have said he has a duty, as the IPCC's chairman, to preserve its impartiality - that the IPCC must not only be neutral, it must be seen to be neutral. But he did not.

On other occasions, he has said that ordinary people should fight climate change by skipping meat one day a week. He has declared that the brakes must be put on what he perceives to be wasteful Western lifestyles. In the words of the UK's *Guardian* newspaper:

> Hotel guests should have their electricity monitored; hefty aviation taxes should be introduced to deter people from flying; and iced water in restaurants should be curtailed...Rajendra Pachauri...warned that western society must undergo a **radical value shift** if the worst effects of climate change were to be avoided. A **new value system**...was now urgently required, he said. [bold added]

Radical value shift. New value system. Are these appropriate topics of conversation for the head of a scientific body? Since when did it become the purview of scientific organizations to tell the public what its values should be?

When did scientists become the new priesthood? (Normally the only people who presume to tell others what they should eat are medical professionals and spiritual leaders.)

Speaking of those large aviation taxes Pachauri thinks are necessary to discourage other people from flying, the Yale interview mentioned, in passing, Pachauri's own habits in that regard:

> He was on yet another stop of what certainly must be one of the most hectic travel schedules on the planet. When

we saw him, Pachauri was in the midst of a trip that was taking him from China, to the United States, to Europe, to Africa, and then back to China, all within a few weeks.

In a world in which teleconferencing has become steadily cheaper what kind of example is Pachauri setting? Does he really intend to send the message that only the little people should stop flying?

Why isn't he calling on celebrities who travel by private jet to make sacrifices for the sake of the planet (Oprah, Leonardo DiCaprio, Arnold Schwarzenegger, that means you) rather than saying it should be more expensive for kids to visit their grandparents during summer vacation?

Perhaps Pachauri is too busy scolding world leaders, instead. In January 2009 he declared in a speech that the emissions targets of incoming President Obama "need to be strengthened." In October of that year a news article was accorded the headline: *Obama 'ought to do a lot more' on climate: Pachauri.*

In the previous chapter I discussed the views of the late Edward Goldsmith, the founder and editor of *The Ecologist* magazine. To be fair, Pachauri doesn't share Goldsmith's open disdain for democracy. During an interview in late 2007, he declared that: "any democracy is 10 times better than what you have in China." Pachauri is also less hostile to technology.

But in other respects, his views are identical to Goldsmith's. Both men think humanity's survival depends on living "in harmony with nature." (How does one live in harmony with poison ivy, a drought, a sandstorm, or an earthquake?) Both believe the proper role of government is not to represent the aspirations of the public, but to redesign society, to dramatically alter people's everyday lives.

According to Pachauri, a "rapid transformation of the economic system" is required. Government "must redefine cultural patterns" and major lifestyles changes must occur *everywhere*. [note 25-1] Affluent countries, he says, "can't continue to consume at this level." And then there's this beauty:

We have been so drunk with this desire to produce and consume more and more whatever the cost to the environment that we're on a totally unsustainable path. I am not going to rest easy until I have articulated in every possible forum the need to bring about major structural changes in economic growth and development. **That's the real issue. Climate change is just a part of it**. [bold added]

Pardon me? Climate change is part of *what*? Let's read those sentences again. According to Pachauri the real issue is bringing about *major structural changes in economic growth and development*. Responding to climate change is merely one aspect of a much larger plan.

I am not making this up. The above quote may be found in a 5,000-word profile of Pachauri that appeared in *Nature*. Considered one of the world's most prestigious scientific publications, in late 2007 it named Pachauri 'newsmaker of the year.'

According to Gabrielle Walker, the author of that profile, during normal conversation Pachauri constantly refers to 'the cause.' Despite her PhD in chemistry, Walker seems not the least bit perturbed by this.

Pachauri has been head of the IPCC since 2002. This means that a supposedly neutral body, entrusted with evaluating scientific evidence in an objective and evenhanded manner, has been run for the past decade by a man who makes no secret of the fact that he regards alarm over climate change as a means to an end.

His real goal is transforming the world's economy.

Pachauri is entitled to pursue whatever objectives make sense to him. But if you want to restructure the global economy you should argue that case on its own merits. It's sneaky and dishonest to accomplish this via the back door, under the guise of responding to an environmental crisis.

26 – FOLLOWING THE LEADER

The harm inflicted on the IPCC by the fact that its own chairman is anything but policy-neutral should not be under-estimated. On an ongoing basis, Pachauri is signaling to the organization he leads that the promises the IPCC makes to the public aren't worth the paper they're written on. He's signaling that it's OK to describe yourself in one way and to behave in quite another.

Big surprise, then, that other IPCC-affiliated scientists have also crossed this line. Rather than sticking scrupulously to their own field of expertise these scientists have publicly thrown their weight behind policies they think should be adopted to fight climate change. Emissions reduction is the big one.

As I've argued above, this is undemocratic. It prevents the entire community from taking part in the debate. It falsely implies that it's the role of scientists to not merely diagnose the problem, but to choose our precise response as well.

Thomas Stocker is a climate modeler from Switzerland. Following 10 years of IPCC involvement, in 2008 he became co-chair of Working Group 1. Each IPCC working group has two chairpersons - one from an affluent country and one from a developing nation. Informally, everyone understands that the former is the person in charge (partly because that individual's government has committed to housing and funding the working group's administrative activities until that edition of the Climate Bible is complete).

Because Stocker is head of the 'science' section of the Climate Bible and his co-chair is from China, his influence in the current IPCC configuration is difficult to overstate.

In 2009 Stocker gave a media interview in which he declared that "all societies on this planet" would have to adopt "a clear schedule of emission reductions." Every sector of the economy, he said, should "contribute to the *grand goal* of decarbonizing society" (my italics).

All societies on the planet. Does that include those who are barely feeding themselves. Really? He expects people concerned about the stunted growth of the children in their arms today to worry about CO_2 emissions that might cause a problem 100 years from now?

In another interview that same year Stocker sounded for all the world like a politician when he opined that the upcoming UNFCCC climate summit:

> must clearly set down the reductions expected from industrialised countries, and at the same time define sanctions if these reduction targets are not met...then we need a clear plan for the way in which emissions allowances are traded.

Let us be clear about what's going on here. This man has decided that humanity's primary response to climate change should be emissions cuts. He's also decided that penalties will be necessary for countries that don't meet their targets. Moreover, he's decided there should be an emissions trading system.

What I want to know is this: Which part of his physics training equips him to make these policy decisions on behalf of the rest of us?

In June 2011, Stocker told a Canadian newspaper that tripling the price of gasoline could help save the planet. According to the *Vancouver Sun*, Stocker believes:

> Much higher pump prices would help people realize there are "much smarter ways to go from point A to point B"

than climbing into "three tonnes of steel and rubber" that spew greenhouse gases...

Neither Stocker, nor the journalist who wrote the story, thought it important to discuss what effect such a price increase might have on families struggling to pay their bills - or on farmers whose tractors run on gasoline.

Jonathan Overpeck is also prominent in the IPCC. He holds a PhD in geological sciences and, during the preparation of the 2007 edition of the Climate Bible, served in five separate IPCC capacities – including leading an important chapter. (It is, no doubt, a total coincidence that one of the contributing authors for that same chapter is Overpeck's wife, Julia Cole.)

Does Overpeck stick to the science, allowing the rest of us to come to our own conclusions? Nope. In 2009 he told a committee of the US Congress that two actions were necessary to avert a water crisis in the Lower Colorado River Basin. One was $200 million in new science funding to study the matter. The other was *worldwide* emissions cuts:

global emissions of greenhouse gases, and especially carbon dioxide, must be reduced significantly. Reductions of greenhouse gas emissions by 2050 to levels 80 percent below 1990 levels is a good target.

Reality check time. That combination of dates and numbers has nothing to do with geology. It is a political goal that is promoted by political activists. [note 26-1]

Secondly, how can this advice be considered remotely sensible? Does anyone seriously believe that browbeating billions of other human beings in other countries into radically altering the way they heat, cook, and get around is the best way to save a US river basin? Does anyone seriously believe the rest of the world will – or should – care about that basin? A more extreme example of American self-absorption is surely difficult to imagine.

The extent to which Overpeck and his wife - who are both members of the University of Arizona's geosciences faculty - now talk politics in their geology courses is suggested by a

May 2010 class that examined "climate misunderstandings and communication." They invited Max Boykoff, an out-of-town guest speaker, to address the course they were jointly teaching. According to a university-issued press release, Boykoff had told journalism students the previous evening that news outlets should refrain from reporting the views of climate skeptics since this contributes to "illusory, misleading and counterproductive debates" that "poorly serve the collective good."

The press release quoted Overpeck in this context, saying that "special interests are working overtime to confuse the public on the science."

Politicians routinely denigrate their opponents by saying they represent *special interests* - but is that how scientists should talk? Religious zealots routinely speak of *the truth* that cannot be questioned - but is it appropriate for geologists to speak about *the science* in a similar manner?

Back when he was earning his PhD, which textbook left Overpeck with the impression that geologists should care how many different perspectives the media presents on an issue? Would it be appropriate for journalists to tell him how to calibrate his microscope?

In the 21st century ordinary people are considered competent enough to choose their own leaders. They're considered smart enough to determine the guilt or innocence of accused murderers. Yet a certain group of 'experts' believe these same people can't be trusted to sort wheat from chaff where climate change is concerned. Apparently, the notion that the public should be shielded from certain climate perspectives now gets discussed in geology class.

One would think that if IPCC personnel really believed the planet was at risk of turning into a fireball they'd be more circumspect. One would expect them to stick carefully to their narrow scientific specialty so that no one would have any excuse to doubt their findings.

But that's not how these people behave. Nor does the IPCC demand it of them. The Chris Landsea story is a case in point.

A Florida-based hurricane expert, Landsea served as a contributing author and expert reviewer on both the 1995 and 2001 editions of the Climate Bible. In late 2004 he was once again invited to write a brief section on hurricanes. The invitation was issued by the person in charge of the relevant IPCC chapter of what would become the 2007 Climate Bible - Kevin Trenberth.

In a recent interview Trenberth was described as a "climate modeler and IPCC insider." Both Landsea and Trenberth are meteorologists. But Landsea's entire career has focussed on hurricanes. Trenberth's has not.

A few weeks after Landsea was contacted, he was surprised to hear that Trenberth intended to participate in a telephone press conference that would claim *experts* believe global warming will *continue* to spur "more outbreaks of intense hurricane activity."

Landsea sent an e-mail addressed jointly to Trenberth and a second colleague, Linda Mearns (who chose not to participate in the subsequent press conference perhaps due to Landsea's concerns). Pointedly, Landsea observed that neither they - nor the three other people scheduled to participate in the press conference - had ever published a research paper on the relationship between hurricanes and climate change. The implication was clear: how could these people claim expertise in that field?

Speaking as the *bona fide* expert, Landsea's e-mail provided a brief overview of this topic. It began with this declaration: "There are no known scientific studies that show a conclusive physical link between global warming and hurricane frequency and intensity."

Despite Landsea's efforts to discourage him, Trenberth went ahead with the press conference. 2004 had been a busy hurricane season in the US and the media was happy to report that people claiming to be experts saw a global warming connection.

The Reuters news story, for example, declared that the "four hurricanes that bashed Florida and the Caribbean within a five-week period over the summer...are only the beginning." The journalist seemed not to notice that the first person quoted in her story - Paul Epstein - is, in fact, a medical doctor - not someone whose professional life has been devoted to the study of hurricanes.

(As for the suggestion that 2004 was *only the beginning*, after Hurricane Katrina devastated New Orleans in 2005, the number of strong hurricanes making landfall in the US promptly plunged. Since then people have begun talking about the unusual 'hurricane drought.')

Following the press conference, Landsea protested Trenberth's actions in an e-mail cc'd to Trenberth and addressed to 15 senior colleagues and IPCC personnel. Among them was chairman Pachauri. Landsea provided a hyperlink to an on-line recording of the entire press conference. In his opinion, the media hadn't exaggerated. Rather, the news stories were consistent with what Trenberth had actually said.

So where, asked Landsea, are the peer-reviewed publications

> that substantiate these pronouncements? What studies are being alluded to that have shown a connection between observed warming trends on the earth and long-term trends in tropical cyclone activity? As far as I know there are none.

Landsea said he was gravely concerned that since Trenberth had already "come to the conclusion that global warming has altered hurricane activity," and since Trenberth would be overseeing the hurricane section in the Climate Bible, "it may not be possible for the IPCC process to proceed objectively."

Landsea then made a perfectly reasonable request. "I would like assurance," he said, "that what will be included in the IPCC report will reflect the best available information and the consensus *within the scientific community most expert on the specific topic*" (my italics).

Landsea's e-mail was dated November 5th, 2004. It would be a full two weeks before he received a reply from Pachauri, who explained that travel to Korea and Australia had prevented him from responding sooner. (In an alternate universe, the IPCC chair might have said the delay was due to the fact that he had required time to investigate matters carefully.)

Rather than acknowledging that Trenberth's behavior had placed the IPCC in an awkward position, Pachauri was dismisssive:

I need hardly mention that the IPCC cannot possibly take a position on this, because individual scientists can do what they wish in their own rights, as long as they are not saying anything on behalf of the IPCC. I may also mention that often the media does exaggerate what scientists may put forward on a balanced and objective basis.

It was clear that Pachauri - whose first priority should surely be the safeguarding of the IPCC's reputation - had not bothered to listen to the recording of the press conference. Had he done so he would have discovered that Trenberth was introduced as a senior author of the IPCC's upcoming report. He would have heard Trenberth himself say: "I was a lead author on the 2001 IPCC report...and in fact I was involved in developing some of the information that is in that report dealing with hurricanes."

What Pachauri would not have heard was a disclaimer that made it clear Trenberth and his colleagues were speaking as private individuals - and that their opinions should in no way be confused with those of the IPCC. It would have taken only 10 seconds to utter such a disclaimer, but that didn't happen.

As the press release issued at the time makes clear, both Trenberth and another speaker were deliberately identified by their IPCC roles. They weren't just anyone making claims about hurricanes and global warming - they were UN-recognized experts.

(Incidentally, James J. McCarthy, the other speaker overtly linked to the IPCC in the press release, was described as "a biological oceanographer at Harvard University and lead author of the climate change impacts portion" of the IPCC's 2001 report. What that description glosses over is that this marine biologist was actually a senior IPCC official between 1997 and 2001. Indeed, he served as co-chair of the IPCC's Working Group 2 for the 2001 Climate Bible.

So it wasn't just Trenberth who was blurring the lines between personal opinions and official IPCC views. McCarthy was, in fact, the much bigger IPCC fish. It does the IPCC no credit that someone as senior as McCarthy would participate in a press conference about a purported link between global warming and more intense hurricanes – even though he has no expertise in that field, and even though no peer-reviewed scientific literature supported his position.)

But let us return to Pachauri's response. The IPCC chairman chose to interpret Landsea's complaint as being about what IPCC-affiliated authors are (or are not) allowed to say in public. That is an important question, but Landsea's main concern was about something else: How can people - whether they be IPCC participants or members of the public - have confidence in the IPCC's neutrality when the person in charge of the chapter that deals with hurricanes expresses opinions at a press conference that flatly contradict the research findings of genuine experts in the field?

Trenberth's return e-mail to Landsea does not appear to be in the public domain, so it's unclear what he said, precisely. What we do know is that Pachauri backed him up 100%. He told Landsea:

> I, therefore, agree entirely with Dr. Trenberth's response to your communication since what he said did not in any way misrepresent the IPCC and *apparently* his statements accurately reflected [the IPCC's 2001 Climate Bible.] (my italics)

Please note that crucial word: apparently. It would seem that the chairman of the IPCC was so indifferent to the implications of this very serious matter that not only did he fail to listen to the press conference, he didn't bother to consult the 2001 Climate Bible himself.

Landsea's response to Pachauri (which was copied to the others to whom he had originally appealed) pointed out that since he'd helped write the section on hurricanes that appeared in the 2001 Climate Bible he knew firsthand that Trenberth's views were *not* an accurate reflection of what that document said. He then quoted chapter and verse for Pachauri's benefit, making it clear that, in 2001, the IPCC had concluded that nothing out of the ordinary appeared to be happening with regard to hurricane frequency or intensity.

Landsea's clear-sighted, dignified resignation from the IPCC is one of the few bright spots in this entire tale. Recognizing that politics was running roughshod over science, Landsea's response to Pachauri, dated December 8, 2004, ended with the following:

> the refereed literature in my field and the consensus by the folks active in [studying] tropical cyclone climate variability conclude the opposite to what Dr. Trenberth is advocating publicly.

> ...Because of Dr. Trenberth's pronouncements the IPCC process...is compromised and its objectivity lost...the IPCC did select Dr. Trenberth as a [coordinating] Lead Author and entrusted him to carry out this duty in a non-biased, objective point of view. To this he has failed. I personally cannot in good faith continue to contribute to a process that I view as not being scientifically sound. As long as this structure remains, I will no longer participate in the IPCC...

27 – MORAL MIDGETS

If there's one thing that can be said about Rajendra Pachauri's chairmanship of the IPCC, it's that he never misses an opportunity to disappoint. The fact that he performed so inadequately with regard to the Landsea affair does not, by now, come as a surprise.

But that still leaves the other scientists who were party to the Landsea-Pachauri correspondence. All of these people were fully aware of the series of events described above. So what was their response? How many of them sided with Landsea? How many continued to participate in the IPCC despite the disturbing things this incident revealed about that organization?

Susan Solomon, the co-chair of Working Group 1 for that edition of the Climate Bible, was amongst the people to whom Landsea appealed. We met her earlier. She's the individual who, in 2005, threatened to expel Steve McIntyre when he tried to do a conscientious job as an IPCC expert reviewer.

Landsea's first e-mail was dispatched on November 5, 2004. What appears to be Solomon's only response to him is dated December 9th - the day after he declared he could no longer participate in the IPCC because he viewed it as scientifically unsound.

Solomon copied her response to everyone who'd received Landsea's original e-mail plus one other person - Martin Manning. He was the head of Working Group 1's technical support unit - the gent who would later tell McIntyre he wasn't in the business of providing secretarial services to expert reviewers.

If anyone wonders where such an arrogant, disrespectful attitude came from, the manner in which Solomon dealt with the Landsea affair a year earlier may be viewed as setting a particular tone. When she sent this e-mail she wasn't speaking solely to Landsea - she was making a statement to everyone with whom Landsea had shared his concerns.

Declaring that she was writing in her capacity as co-chair of Working Group 1, Solomon brushed aside Landsea's strongly-held view that Trenberth had presented himself as an IPCC expert at the hurricane press conference. According to Solomon:

> when you or I are introduced as [National Oceanic and Atmospheric Administration] scientists, it is well understood that we are not speaking for NOAA much less the US government. That is **standard practice** in scientific work in all institutions and organizations. [bold added]

But the IPCC isn't just any organization. Governments around the world point to the Climate Bible as the reason they're spending billions of dollars, are introducing new taxes, and are initiating tough new regulations regarding everything from delivery trucks to light bulbs to building codes.

President Obama's science advisor says the IPCC produces the "most important conclusions" about climate change. The media tells us the IPCC is a *gold standard* organization. Surely, therefore, we have a right to expect more than *standard practice* from those involved.

Solomon could have taken steps to prevent similar future misunderstandings by acknowledging that Landsea had a point. She could have telegraphed to her entire working group, especially the people who were party to the Landsea e-mail conversation, that anyone who is an IPCC author really should preface their public remarks with a 10-second disclaimer making it clear they are not speaking for the IPCC. This easy, no-cost solution was readily available. Had Solomon adopted it Landsea might have reconsidered his decision to quit the IPCC. But she didn't give him even that.

As for his concern that Trenberth's public remarks called into question the impartiality with which the hurricane section would be written, Solomon brushed this aside, too. Her comments are worth examining closely because they provide important insight into the mindset of IPCC movers and shakers:

> as you know, the publication date of the fourth assessment report will be 2007. I would like to suggest that it is quite clear that no person can speak on behalf of that assessment's scientific conclusions until it is available.

> While different scientists involved in climate studies have different views, the assessment will represent, as in the [2001 report], a careful consensus based upon consideration of published scientific literature. It will, as in [the 2001 report], include consideration of observed frequency and intensity changes as well as available modelling studies. The authors of chapter 3 will weigh all relevant papers and come to a consensus as a group, with important input from an extensive review process. I am confident that the process will be a diligent one.

First, Solomon dismisses the bias concern by pointing to the fact the Climate Bible won't be published until 2007. But how would she herself feel if, prior to her appearance before a judge to discuss a parking ticket, the judge declared at a press conference that the vast majority of those ticketed are obviously guilty? If the evidence pointed to her innocence, and she lodged a complaint about the judge being biased, would she have been comforted to hear that since her trial was still months away nothing was yet set in stone?

Solomon told Landsea that those writing the IPCC hurricane chapter would take into account the scientific literature *as well as modeling studies*. Translation: even if all the scientific literature based on *real-world observations* says one thing, modeling studies may well say something else.

While Landsea had sought assurance that the IPCC's hurricane findings would reflect the consensus of experts *in that field*, Solomon advised him that, after considering input from a range of people, the IPCC authors would *come to a consensus as a group*. Translation: forget what genuine experts in a particular field believe to be true. The truth is whatever IPCC personnel say it is.

According to the co-chair of the working group that deals with the 'hard science' portion of the Climate Bible, this is how IPCC chapters get written. The IPCC feels no need to reflect - or respect - the views of actual experts. Instead, the IPCC places decision-making power in the hands of non-experts.

This is the time to remind ourselves that many IPCC authors aren't chosen for their scientific prowess. They're graduate students, affirmative action selections, activists, and virtual reality climate modelers. That, ladies and gentleman, is how the IPCC arrives at its 'gold standard' science.

Personally, I wouldn't spend $500 on the advice of a report that had been prepared in such a manner. The notion that leaders of wealthy and important nations are proposing to spend trillions on climate change measures on the say-so of this kind of report makes me think we've all lost our minds.

But let us turn our attention to the other scientists who had front-row seats at this sorry affair, the people with whom Landsea chose to share his concerns. Four of them hold senior positions with US government agencies, but appear to have steered clear of the IPCC altogether. Three more are from China, The Gambia, and Iran - countries in which it cannot be assumed that they were at liberty to make their own decisions.

But that still leaves six scientists (in addition to Pachauri, Solomon, Manning and Trenberth) who continued their IPCC association despite what had just transpired. Brian Hoskins, Phil Jones, Thomas Karl, and Albert Klein Tank all remained involved in the hurricane chapter. Thomas Peterson and Linda Mearns continued their involvement with other chapters. In total, Hoskins served in four separate IPCC capacities, Karl in two. [note 27-1]

There are moments in this life when our decisions really, truly matter - when, by our actions, we demonstrate the quality of our character. If we believe in impartiality, we must speak up. If we believe in scientific integrity, we must defend it.

Chris Landsea did exactly this. That he was surrounded by people apparently incapable of recognizing the wider implications of the situation he'd brought to their attention should give us all pause.

The moral failure here was profound. And it didn't end with this small group of scientists. Landsea resigned from the IPCC in December 2004. The following January he went public in the form of an 'open letter to the community' sent to 45 colleagues - one of whom then posted it on the Internet.

Landsea said he hoped, via his open letter, to raise awareness about "what I view as a problem in the IPCC process." After describing the series of events, he wrote:

> It is beyond me why my colleagues would utilize the media to push an unsupported agenda that recent hurricane activity has been due to global warming. Given Dr. Trenberth's role as the IPCC's [coordinating] Lead Author responsible for preparing the text on hurricanes, his public statements so far outside of current scientific understanding led me to concern that it would be very difficult for the IPCC process to proceed objectively with regards to the assessment on hurricane activity.
>
> ...I was disappointed when the IPCC leadership dismissed my concerns...

Along with his open letter, Landsea attached the e-mails he'd sent on this matter - and the ones he'd received in response from Pachauri and Solomon. There was no need to take his word for it, a clear record of what had occurred was available.

News outlets should have run with this story. It should have become a full-fledged scandal. If an organization that everyone thinks is producing authoritative *scientific* reports has been compromised by those advancing a scientifically unsupported position surely this is an important development. If the leadership of the IPCC is exhibiting a bunker mentality by refusing to even acknowledge there's a problem, surely the public deserves to know.

The *Washington Post* story provided the basic details and even quoted Landsea at some length. But the journalist then trivialized the matter by characterizing it as a "spat between Landsea and Trenberth" - before observing that IPCC officials had declined to intervene in the *dispute*.

For its part *Science* magazine (which is published by the American Association for the Advancement of Science), devoted one-third of a single page in its three-page *News of the Week* section to the matter. In the judgment of the magazine's staff, this story deserved to appear last - after articles that discussed the merger of two agricultural research bodies in the developing world, NASA budget cuts, funding for science education in Sub-Saharan Africa, and the announcement of an annual $1 million donation to the Arab Science and Technology Foundation.

On the page in which the story finally appeared, a controversy involving a biology lab at Boston University received top billing and twice as much space.

Science's account of the Landsea affair began with this line: "An ugly spat has broken out among contributors to the world's leading scientific report on climate change." The next paragraph characterized the matter as a *tussle*. That story included a new quote from Pachauri, reiterating that IPCC authors are "free to express their views on any subject."

What's astonishing is that no one - not the three writers involved, nor anyone else at *Science*, connected the dots despite the damning nature of the remarks that appeared at the end of the story. We're told that Trenberth

defended his view that changing sea conditions could be contributing to greater hurricane intensity.

That position is "plausible," says hurricane expert Kerry Emanuel of the Massachusetts Institute of Technology.

But hurricane activity varies so much from decade to decade that **"not a single person in my field thinks you can see the signal**." [bold added]

If not a single hurricane expert thinks there's a link between hurricanes and global warming, how can it possibly be OK for an IPCC senior author who is not a hurricane expert to make statements to the contrary at a press conference? This is not a question of two competing schools of thought amongst people with roughly equal credentials. This is a case in which someone with no expertise was promulgating his personal opinion directly to the media and enhancing that opinion by pointing to his IPCC affiliation.

How could the IPCC permit such a person to remain in charge of the hurricane section at what we've been told is the world's preeminent science body? How could its senior officials be so blinkered and unprofessional? Did their mothers never tell them that respect cannot be commanded - it must be earned?

The media coverage was wholly inadequate, but this story did get reported. Large numbers of people involved in the IPCC became aware of these events. Yet no letters-to-the-editor of *Science*, signed by groups of concerned scientists, protested Trenberth's behavior - or Pachauri and Solomon's pathetic response. Nor did people resign *en masse* from the IPCC. To my knowledge there were no other resignations, period.

This tells us something important about the judgment of the scientific community that expects us to trust that exact same judgment on the question of whether global warming is the fault of human beings.

And it says something about the decision, two years later, to award the IPCC a Nobel Peace Prize. Apparently, that prize is now given to moral midgets.

28 – SPINNING STRAW INTO GOLD

In January 2005 *Science* reported that not a single hurricane expert saw any link between hurricanes and global warming. (As I write this in mid-2011, considerable research continues to find no connection.) Although it was unlikely the world's hurricane experts would have done a 180-degree turn on this question during the time period in which the 2007 Climate Bible was being written, this did not discourage the IPCC from talking up the hurricane threat.

Scientists usually refer to hurricanes as cyclones and these were discussed not only in Kevin Trenberth's chapter but in a *dozen* others as well. The reason for this is straightforward: even though hurricane experts say there's no evidence that global warming will make cyclones worse, IPCC personnel nevertheless *believe* this will be the case. Why? Because climate models say so.

Climate models are a collection of assumptions and educated guesses about how the real world behaves. If you're thinking that this kind of circular logic is almost as scary as a cyclone, you're not alone. IPCC personnel believe cyclones will intensify because models programmed by people who believe they'll intensify tell them so.

The Climate Bible devotes an entire section to discussing how recent climate model studies confirm earlier climate model studies that say "future tropical cyclones would likely become more severe" in a warming world. Another section discusses the contradictory results produced by attempts to simulate cyclone activity - as well as the deficiencies associated with both climate models and our current level of scientific understanding.

Nevertheless that section ends with a declaration that human activities *"more likely than not* have contributed to an increase in tropical cyclone intensity" (my italics). This, of course, is an opinion. It is an opinion sharply at odds with the one held by genuine hurricane experts. But the two people in charge of the chapter in which this declaration was made are climate modelers - and in the land of the IPCC they rule.

When the Climate Bible's summary of summaries advised world leaders in three places that the IPCC believes global warming will increase the intensity of hurricanes, no mention was made of the fact that hurricane experts dispute this. [note 28-1] This is what cross-examining lawyer Jason Johnston means when he says the Climate Bible advances a point-of-view rather than presenting all the relevant facts.

But that's only the beginning of the IPCC's controversial treatment of natural disasters. Roger Pielke Jr. is an environmental studies professor at the University of Colorado in Boulder. He thinks human-caused climate change is a concern and that we should invest in technologies that will decarbonize our energy supply. Nevertheless, in recent years he has become an IPCC critic.

Pielke follows research on natural disasters closely and says that, so far, there is no discernible connection between human CO_2 emissions and extreme weather events. Floods, droughts, and hurricanes have always occurred. Pielke says if you look at the long term, big picture there is no convincing evidence they are becoming more frequent or more severe.

In 2009 a seriously irritated Pielke wrote a blog post titled *Systematic Misrepresentation of the Science of Disasters and Climate Change*. "I have seen some disturbing things take place in the scientific community," he declared, and "where I have observed the most shenanigans is the area in which I have considerable expertise."

His blog post described a pattern of shoddy scholarship on the part of those who argue that a link has been established between human-caused climate change and natural disasters. For example, the 2001 edition of the Climate Bible claimed that climate change was responsible for a portion of the damages caused by recent natural disasters. But it is being charitable to describe the basis of this claim as flimsy. The IPCC's supporting evidence was a non-peer-reviewed report that, says Pielke, provided little hard data, failed to describe its methodology, and came to no solid conclusions.

The report was prepared by an insurance company. This is an industry that stands to benefit financially - via higher premiums - if society comes to believe that climate change will cause more disasters. Because the insurance industry is not a disinterested party, by no means should informal speculation in one of its publications be mistaken for sound science.

Nevertheless, the IPCC spun straw into gold. In the eyes of its authors, inconclusive findings became persuasive evidence. It is more than a little troubling that one of the authors of the insurance report, Gerhard Berz, was also a lead author for the IPCC chapter where this occurred. Another party to that decision was Laurens Bouwer, whom we met in the early pages of this book. He was a lead author for this chapter even though he was only a trainee who had yet to complete his Masters degree.

Since 2001, therefore, IPCC officials have insisted it's an established fact that emissions-triggered climate change is adding to disaster costs. Even worse, this IPCC finding has taken on a life of its own.

Pielke points out that a 2005 commentary in *Science*, authored by US-government scientist Evan Mills, linked climate change to rising disaster costs. *Science* is considered a reputable journal that publishes high quality information, but those paying close attention noticed that Mills cited the 2001 Climate Bible and the insurance company report as his main evidence - leaving the impression that these were **a)** solid sources of information and **b)** separate lines of evidence. From that time forward there was now an article in the peer-reviewed literature that could be pointed to to support the general argument.

In June 2009 a 196-page report about climate change impacts was delivered to the US Congress. On page seven Obama's science advisor, John Holdren, said the report had been prepared by an "expert team of scientists" who deserved to be commended for "the outstanding quality of their work." Mills was one of the authors of this report - as was James McCarthy (the former IPCC official who participated in the Trenberth hurricane press conference) and Jonathan Overpeck (who invites guest speakers into his geology classes to argue that the media should pretend climate skeptics don't exist). Among the report's "blue ribbon reviewers" was the same Susan Solomon who'd rejected Landsea's concerns out-of-hand.

In Pielke's words, this report treats the Mills *Science* article "as the definitive source" on the question of disaster costs and climate change. Pielke says that, in order to make its case, the US report also cites non-peer-reviewed work by Mills while ignoring "relevant peer reviewed research showing different results." Finally, he says, Mills' resume lists more than 30 entities for which he has served as a consultant. The fact that many of those entities might wish to influence US climate and energy policy raises conflict-of-interest concerns.

So a dubious finding that originated in a document written by an insurance company was included in the Climate Bible in 2001. It then made its way into the peer-reviewed scientific literature in 2005. By 2009 it was being treated as gospel by a US government report. Welcome to the confidence-inspiring world of climate science.

But Pielke's concerns extend further. Those who believe hurricanes are getting worse point to the fact that the cost of the economic damage inflicted by them has risen in recent years. But more people live near coastlines than they used to, and their homes are now larger and more expensive. Therefore, when a hurricane strikes, the cost of setting things right is higher.

As Pielke explains: "Once disaster data are adjusted for growth and development - everywhere that people have looked, US, Europe, Asia, Australia, Central America, India" the additional costs are fully accounted for. There is no evidence that greenhouse gas emissions have anything to do with the matter. Pielke says plenty of peer-reviewed work has been done on this topic and the results are "not ambiguous."

To Pielke's dismay, when the 2007 Climate Bible was released its summary paragraph about disaster costs began by highlighting a single paper that suggested the exact opposite.

Pielke was familiar with that one paper since it was prepared for a May 2006 workshop he'd helped organize. (Remember IPCC chairman Pachauri's written assurance that the 2007 Climate Bible "was based on scientific studies completed *before* January 2006"? How do we explain the fact that although this workshop paper missed that cutoff date by several months, it was nevertheless cited by Chapters 1, 6, and 7 of the Working Group 2 report?)

Twenty-four papers were presented at Pielke's workshop, spanning a range of analyses and opinions. In the end, after two days of discussion and debate, the participants jointly agreed to a series of consensus statements that acknowledged it isn't possible to link storm damages to human greenhouse gas emissions - and likely won't be anytime soon. [note 28-2]

Ignoring this consensus, the IPCC instead built its entire argument around a particular section of a single paper that suggested otherwise. In Pielke's words, the IPCC appeared to be reaching for anything it could find "to support a conclusion that simply is not backed up in the broader literature." The IPCC attempted, he said, to "overturn the robust conclusions of an entire literature" by highlighting one non-peer-reviewed piece of research.

But the shenanigans weren't over. There was still the matter of the mystery graph. When Pielke first discussed this graph on his blog in early 2007 he titled his post *This is Just Embarrassing.* "I have," he wrote, "generally been a supporter of the IPCC, but I do have to admit that if it is this sloppy and irresponsible in an area of climate change where I have expertise, why should I have confidence in the areas where I am not an expert?"

The graph showed two lines - one representing temperature and the other disaster costs. Both trended gently upward. The caption beneath began: "An example from the literature of one study..." It then cited the single paper upon which the IPCC had chosen to hang its hat. [note 28-3]

But nothing like this graph had been included in the paper it was being attributed to. Pielke said he was shocked and amazed that something so flawed had ended up in the Climate Bible. Off the top of his head he thought it suffered from at least seven serious problems.

It would be three years before Pielke fully unraveled the mystery of the graph's origin. Along the way he would discover that Canadian climate modeler Francis Zwiers, in his capacity as an IPCC expert reviewer, had questioned a hurricane claim being made by the IPCC which cast doubt on the findings of three research papers authored by Pielke. Admirably, Zwiers felt that if the IPCC was going to reject the findings of these papers it should explain why. "What does Pielke think about this?" Zwiers asked.

Records show that an unidentified author of that chapter had replied: "I believe Pielke agrees that adding 2004 and 2005 has the potential to change his earlier conclusions..." But no one had actually bothered to ask Pielke. In his words, the IPCC "simply made up a misleading and false response about my views. Not good."

A reader of Pielke's blog began examining other expert reviewer comments for that chapter. It appeared, he wrote in a comment, that an early version had contained a different graph - one that had been criticized by expert reviewers. The authors of the chapter apparently responded to these criticisms by substituting a new one.

Finally, in February 2010, a contributing author of the chapter admitted he had drawn up the new graph "informally."

In Pielke's words: "The IPCC created a graph that did not exist in the peer reviewed literature or in the grey literature to suggest a relationship between increasing temperatures and rising disaster costs."

The IPCC is supposed to survey the existing scientific literature. When it decided to include the mystery graph it faked the evidence.

Cynthia Rosenzweig was one of the two leaders of the chapter in which these events transpired. Rather than being a minor IPCC player, this NASA climate modeler served in six distinct capacities during the preparation of the 2007 Climate Bible. She is, in other words, a member of what I've come to think of as the IPCC Insiders' Club. Australian meteorologist David Karoly was a lead author for that chapter, having worn six IPCC hats himself.

Invented opinion. Faked evidence. The chapter in which the IPCC discussed natural disasters was not a gold standard effort. Sub-standard is more like it. This surely calls into question the numerous other sections of the Climate Bible in which Rosenzweig and Karoly were involved.

29 – THE CUT-AND-PASTE JOB

People frequently describe what the IPCC does as a "literature review." But IPCC reports are called assessments because, after acquainting themselves with all of the available literature, its authors are expected to draw conclusions about what that literature says. In some ways, this is similar to what a jury does in a court case. After listening to different versions of events, the jury decides which one is most likely to be true.

In his 2008 book, Canadian climate modeler Andrew Weaver declared: "The writing of the IPCC assessment reports is without a doubt the most intensive and rigorous scientific process in which I have been involved."

But the mere fact that scientists participate doesn't make a process scientific. Few of us would describe what a jury does as *scientific*. In both instances, evidence is examined and evaluated. The end result depends on the good - or bad – judgment of the human beings who take part.

In court cases, both sides are given the chance to object to jurors who may be incapable of keeping an open mind. A trial involving a fast food company shouldn't have anyone on the jury who works for that company. Nor should the jury include consumer advocates who've been criticizing the company for years. A fair hearing, by people without any preconceived notions, is the goal.

According to Paul Reiter, when the IPCC decided to write about diseases spread by mosquitoes, the result was "amateurish." This suggests that, rather than systematically examining all of the available scientific literature and drawing conclusions based on that literature, preconceived ideas on the part of the IPCC's authors got in the way.

There is, in fact, good reason to conclude this is exactly what happened. In the IPCC's early years, chapters were led by one person rather than two. [note 29-1] The gentleman who served in that capacity for the Climate Bible's first health chapter was an Australian epidemiology professor named Anthony McMichael. (Epidemiology is the study of diseases in a broad context.)

According to a 2001 bio, McMichael's early research interests spanned a considerable range of topics - mental health, occupational diseases, the link between diet and cancer, and environmental epidemiology. In the late 1980s he co-authored a "bestselling guide to a healthier lifestyle" that discussed nutrition and physical fitness.

The bio tells us it was only "during the 1990s" that McMichael developed "a strong interest" in the health risks associated with global environmental change. So in the early 1990s, out of all the experts in the entire world the IPCC might have chosen to oversee the writing of a chapter examining how climate change might impact human health, why was McMichael selected?

I suspect it had a great deal to do with another book he wrote - the one that appeared in 1993 titled *Planetary Overload: Global Environmental Change and the Health of the Human Species*. This book's central theme is that human activity is undermining the planet's ecosystem. Its tone and analysis are similar to hundreds of other environmental treatises published in recent decades.

McMichael declares that "humans cannot live apart from nature, remote from the great web of life." He frets that we are too distant "from the rhythms of natural systems." He speaks of environmental degradation as "an unprecedented moral problem" and says people in rich countries live a wasteful, "ecologically distorted lifestyle."

The language here is not the tentative sort used by dispassionate scientists. Back in 1993 McMichael didn't say there was concern that carbon dioxide *might* eventually "disrupt various of the biosphere's natural cycles." He confidently proclaimed that it *would*. Like Rajendra Pachauri and Edward Goldsmith, McMichael believes environmental challenges require a wholesale "reordering of social values."

In other words, *Planetary Overload* is not a science book. It is a polemic - an argument inviting us to see the world in the eco-alarmist way the author does. McMichael's day job happens to involve the study of public health, but he has no expertise in most of the topics his book discusses.

He is, of course, entitled to his personal opinions. But was he the best choice to lead an IPCC chapter? Let's rephrase that: If one wished to deliberately stack the deck, to ensure that a certain perspective would dominate the Climate Bible's health chapter, would someone who had expressed views similar to McMichael's not have seemed like the perfect candidate?

There is a straight line between what the UN's 1995 Climate Bible told the world about health issues and what McMichael had already written in his 1993 book. *Planetary Overload* isn't included among the 182 references listed at the end of the health chapter. Which is curious, since entire passages of the Climate Bible were lifted directly from it. My research has indentified 11 instances in which the wording in these two documents is almost identical. [note 29-2]

Consider, for example, these two passages:

McMichael's 1993 book, page 154:
In eastern Africa, a relatively small increase in winter temperature would enable the malarial zone to extend 'upwards' to engulf the large urban highland populations that are currently off-limits to the mosquito because of the cooler temperatures at higher altitudes – e.g. Nairobi (Kenya) and Harare (Zimbabwe). Indeed, such populations around the world, currently just outside the margins of endemic malaria, would provide early evidence of climate-related shifts in the distribution of this disease.

Climate Bible's 1995 Working Group 2 report, p. 574:
Hence, it is a reasonable prediction that, in eastern Africa, a relatively small increase in winter temperature could extend the mosquito habitat and thus enable faciparum malaria to reach beyond the usual altitude limit of around 2,500 m to the large, malaria-free urban highland populations, e.g. Nairobi in Kenya and Harare in Zimbabwe. Indeed, the monitoring of such populations around the world, currently just beyond the boundaries of stable enemic malaria, could provide early evidence of climate-related shifts in malaria distribution.

What the IPCC said about malaria in eastern Africa was what McMichael's book had said - with a few extra words inserted. Rather than surveying the large body of work on malaria written by experts who have devoted their lives to the careful study of this disease, this IPCC chapter parroted McMichael's polemical views.

That was problem number one. Problem number two is that the paragraph that appeared in the Climate Bible contains errors. For example, Nairobi is 1,660 meters above sea level - well short of the IPCC's implied 2,500+ meters. Contrary to the IPCC's suggestion that malaria would be new to Nairobi due to climate change, that city (which began as a swamp) was plagued by this disease from the time of its founding at the turn of the century until the 1950s. [note 29-3]

Harare, in Zimbabwe, is only 1,500 meters above sea level - a full 1,000 meters lower than what the Climate Bible implies.

As Reiter pointed out in his 2005 testimony to the British House of Lords, the IPCC had already decided, back in 1995, that climate change could be blamed for the spread of malaria. But the sole piece of evidence for this assertion was an article written by people who weren't experts that was published in a general interest, popular science magazine. [note 29-4] That's right, folks - a single, non-peer-reviewed magazine article was all the proof the IPCC needed.

This is the same phenomenon that, in the previous chapter, Roger Pielke Jr. complained about. Rather than accurately reflecting the view of *bona fide* experts and the findings of large amounts of scientific work, the IPCC cherry picks outrageously. The result is that the picture it presents to the world bears little relationship to reality.

Reiter also objected to the fact that much of the Climate Bible's discussion of mosquito-borne diseases involved predictions generated by computer models. These predictions, he said, were "based on a highly simplistic model" designed for a totally different purpose. Nevertheless, the IPCC declared that, according to model projections, the percentage of the world's population at risk of malaria would increase from 45% to 60% by the second half of the 21st century.

This is a good time to point out that it was only in 1967 that the World Health Organization declared Poland malaria-free. The Netherlands achieved that designation in 1970. Large parts of the world managed to eradicate malaria during the 20th century. Yet despite this clear historical trend, the IPCC implausibly wants us to believe the percentage of humanity at risk of this disease will increase during the 21st.

In Reiter's words, the treatment of malaria by the IPCC "was ill-informed, biased, and scientifically unacceptable." But the news media had no way of knowing this. Not only did it report the IPCC's conclusion that climate change was going to lead to more malaria, it distorted matters further.

Erroneously characterizing mosquito-borne diseases as tropical illnesses the UK's *Independent* newspaper announced, in October 1995, that:

> The consensus of 2,000 top meteorologists and other experts consulted by the IPCC is that tropical diseases will increasingly spread into temperate areas...

In fact, only 21 people worked on the chapter that dealt with mosquito-borne diseases. Two thousand souls did not even *discuss* this matter, never mind arrive at a consensus about it.

30 – STEERING SOCIETY

Anthony McMichael's leading of the 1995 health chapter was merely the beginning of this public health professor's career with the IPCC. During the planning stages for the 2001 edition of the Climate Bible, the IPCC adopted a practice of pairing a first-world convening author with a developing-world convening lead author. McMichael was once again tapped to lead the health chapter, together with Andrew Githeko, a researcher from Kenya. [note 30-1] When it came time to write the next Climate Bible update, released in 2007, McMichael was selected for a third time, albeit for a smaller role.

Public health is a branch of medicine that has long been associated with crusaders who scold the rest of us about how much we eat, drink, and weigh. It's worth calling attention to this fact before we look at some of the other people who helped write the 1995 IPCC health chapter - the document that Paul Reiter says was responsible for promulgating far and wide the misleading ideas about malaria and climate change that he's still battling today.

In addition to McMichael there were nine other lead authors. Jonathan Patz was mentioned earlier in this book. He qualified as a medical doctor in 1987 and, in 1992, graduated with a Masters in Public Health. According to a 2007 profile, Patz is a former family physician who believes that "The further you can go upstream along the causal chain of disease, the more people you can prevent from getting sick."

Allow me a brief digression. In the late 1990s, the media was full of stories about how the Y2K computer bug would wreak havoc when the year 2000 arrived. In 1997, for example, *Newsweek* magazine ran a headline titled *The Day the World Shuts Down*. In 1998 it published another article that included these lines:

> Mark Andrews, a San Diego doctor, feels so strongly about the impending catastrophe that he has quit his medical practice, moved his family to a farm in a South-western state and begun barnstorming the country giving lectures about Y2K preparedness. "I realized I could save more lives getting people to make contingency plans," he says.

It seems to me there are parallels between doctors such as Andrews and doctors like Patz. [note 30-2]

In 1995, what appears to be Patz's first research paper appeared. It dealt with health risks after surgery. In other words, a mere two years after his Masters graduation, with no relevant publications whatsoever, he somehow became an IPCC lead author. In 2001 he reprised his lead author role with the health chapter and then, somewhat oddly, served as a lead author on the North America chapter for the 2007 edition.

Patz is now described as a "UN IPCC Scientist." [note 30-3] But in interviews he sounds more like an activist. In the 2007 profile, he's quoted as saying:

> Considering that most developing nations are burdened by major infectious diseases and famine, which are highly dependent on climate, these countries are most vulnerable to the global warming that we in the industrialized world are causing. It's a huge ethical problem. One could make the argument that our energy policy is indirectly **exporting diseases** to other parts of the world. [bold added]

Famine and disease have plagued humanity since the beginning of time. Sometimes they are connected to climate, sometimes not. In the 1950s, it was Chinese government policies - not climate - that resulted in the starvation deaths of an estimated 20 million souls. Reiter says malaria is mentioned 13 times in Shakespeare's plays. Anyone who thinks it is the fault of the modern, affluent Western world, that we are *exporting* it to the developing world, is well and truly out there.

Patz, like many other environmentalists, believes we have an "urgent need to end our addiction to fossil fuels" and that we are "using up natural resources at an unsustainable rate." He is entitled to his opinions. But the important question is this: If the Climate Bible is going to be relied on by governments, regulators, judges, and journalists should it not be produced by cool, dispassionate professionals rather than by people whose analysis is indistinguishable from Greenpeace?

In recent years, Patz has co-authored several papers with another medical doctor who, wouldn't you know it, also holds a Masters in public health. His name is Paul Epstein. You may remember him as one of the people who participated in the Kevin Trenberth hurricane press conference in 2004. Back in 1995, he also served as a lead author on the Climate Bible's first health chapter. Unlike Patz, though, Epstein had published extensively prior to joining the IPCC.

But an important caveat is in order. Rather than being a research scientist whose papers impart specialized, in-depth knowledge, Epstein has been closer to a medical journalist. His published work prior to the 1995 Climate Bible dealt with an extensive range of topics - from health issues in Nicaragua, to Kurdish refugees, to Soviet nuclear mishaps. [note 30-4]

Oh, and that magazine article by non-experts that claimed malaria had already spread due to climate change? Epstein was one the people who wrote it. Coincidentally, he was also one of the people who decided, on behalf of the IPCC, that it was sound science. [note 30-5]

Following his contribution to the 1995 Climate Bible, Epstein's published work examined cholera in *west* Africa, disease-causing weeds in *east* Africa, and US drinking water challenges in the 21st century. In 2008 he authored an editorial in a medical journal titled *Fossil fuels, allergies and a host of other ills*. Abandoning all pretense of circumspect scientific reasoning, he indulged in full-throttle political advocacy:

> For social, ecologic, and health reasons, we must wean ourselves from fossil fuels...There are major choices to be made along the path away from fossil fuels. The public health...professions have a key role to play...we can help policymakers and industrial leaders make well informed decisions...we may just be able to help **steer society** onto a path leading to a healthy and sustainable energy future. [bold added]

Once more, therefore, we find that an individual who served as a lead author for the IPCC's health chapter is someone who not only lacks the deep expertise of a Reiter, he also sees the world through an overtly activist lens. By his own admission, Epstein thinks it's the job of people like him to *steer society* down a certain path.

Which brings us, finally, to Alistair Woodward - a New Zealand professor who also began his professional life as a medical doctor with public health training. He holds a PhD in epidemiology and currently heads the University of Auckland's School of Population Health.

Woodward has been involved with every IPCC health chapter that has ever been written. He now leads that chapter for the edition of the Climate Bible expected to be completed in 2013. [note 30-6]

Nearly 20 years ago, in 1994, Anthony "cut-and-paste" McMichael and Woodward published a paper together. It argued that although technology might improve fossil fuel efficiency and reduce pollution, this wouldn't be sufficient to avert the need for "more radical sociopolitical change."

There is, of course, no reason to believe that the world can be re-made in a manner that satisfies green activists. Nations that have tried to impose top-down radical change have oceans of blood on their hands. Human societies are organic. They evolve. Attempts to plan them fail miserably.

The idea that people will start living dramatically differently just because green activists think they should is a young person's fantasy. To quote Roger Pielke Jr., "The vast majority of people simply do not want their lives transformed." Many of them are barely coping as it is. They're struggling to pay their bills, to provide opportunities for their children, and to care for the elderly and disabled. In democratic societies any political party that tries to introduce *radical sociopolitical change* is unlikely to be re-elected. That's the real world.

So have Woodward's views matured over the past two decades? Has he tossed aside the green-tinted glasses and become more moderate? Can the person now at the helm of the health chapter be expected to produce a neutral, unbiased assessment rooted in scientific fact rather than environmental advocacy?

In July 2011 Woodward's online academic bio page listed ten publications of which he is the author or co-author. All are dated 2009 and fully half of them deal with climate change. The first, published in February, discusses carbon pricing. Its connection to either science or medicine is tenuous. The conclusion of that paper declares that "if climate change is not *controlled* through timely *central government* means then health losses will occur worldwide" (my italics).

The final three paragraphs are nothing less than a political rallying cry. Health professionals should discuss, encourage, and support "action on climate change." They should make their views known to a committee examining New Zealand's proposed emissions trading scheme. They should "join in action with other health professionals globally" to prepare for the Copenhagen climate summit.

That the above appeared in *The New Zealand Medical Journal* is astonishing. But alas, this is only the beginning.

Eight months later that same journal published another political screed. Woodward's name is second on a co-author list of 26 people, the vast majority of whom work in public health. This paper says New Zealand should "halve its greenhouse gas emissions by 2020." Moreover, it says, "reducing the risk of *catastrophic* climate change may require deeper cuts" (my italics).

Here it is worth mentioning an opinion piece written for the BBC by a prominent UK climate scientist back in 2006. As director of the Tyndall Centre for Climate Change Research, Mike Hulme believes human activities are linked to global warming - and that action must be taken. But three years prior to this Woodward paper he'd already become concerned about the way activists were distorting the issue. In his words:

> The language of catastrophe is not the language of science...To state that climate change will be "catastrophic" hides a cascade of value-laden assumptions which do not emerge from empirical or theoretical science.

Noting that the tendency to resort to "the language of fear, terror and disaster" has "been seen in other areas of public health risk," he says this sort of language cannot be considered scientifically accurate.

Fear, terror, and disaster just about cover the Woodward paper. It speaks of *runaway climate collapse*, *tipping points*, and *potentially unstoppable* climate change. It says there is a need for "concerted action...before it is too late" and that the situation is *extremely urgent*. It cites four Greenpeace reports and two World Wildlife Fund documents.

Moreover, the authors of this paper declare that fighting climate change will require a "profound reengineering of New Zealand's structure and function."

If the previous Woodward paper ended with a political rallying cry, this one is accompanied by a marching band. Doctors are told they must *mobilise society* because they have a *responsibility to lead*. This is followed by a list of 13 things they should do - sorted into three categories by the authors of the paper. The majority of these suggestions (seven) appear in the *political* category. Two more are in the *personal* category, while another four are labeled *professional*.

The evidence could not be clearer. This is not a paper about medicine. By the authors' own admission, nine of their 13 suggested measures are unrelated to doctors' professional lives.

One of those suggestions, by the way, declares that doctors should educate and encourage their patients *in climate change action*. The day my doctor starts talking about climate change is the day I find myself a professional who understands that the purpose of a medical consultation is to discuss my issues - not hers.

Two of the other climate-related papers on Woodward's list are more moderate, but the last one takes the prize. Its message, in a nutshell, is: *Down with free speech. Thou shalt all think alike.*

Here Woodward and his co-authors declare that: "As a profession and as global citizens, **we need to move beyond dissent and denial**" (bold added). The paper wins the silly-quote-of-the-year award with its insistence that "Change is not necessarily normal." You may find it as amusing as I do that it also declares:

> The climate change deniers have used data selectively [whereas] the IPCC has assiduously used all available data...

In ice hockey, a person who scores three goals in a single game is said to have accomplished a *hat trick* (historically, fans celebrated by throwing their hats on the ice rink). In 2009 the person who now heads the IPCC's health chapter scored his own hat trick. This trio of papers demonstrate an undisguised propensity for political activism. There is no indication in any of them that cool, quiet, scientific facts articulated by experts such as Paul Reiter have a hope of penetrating Woodward's entrenched belief system.

When he became head of his university's School of Population Health in 2004, Woodward used part of his inaugural address to respond to concerns expressed by critics such as Reiter. These remarks are particularly revealing:

> The Reiter group believes the work of the IPCC and its followers is inaccurate, and scientifically misleading. Those of us who are involved with the IPCC argue that the science is fine, it is **the definition of accuracy** that is at issue. The stakes are high. What should be done to reduce CO2 levels, and when, depends on the costs of [doing nothing to prevent] climate change. When such accounts are drawn up, the health impacts are significant items. **If**

diseases like malaria are not a serious concern, then there are fewer compelling reasons to cut carbon emissions. [bold added] [note 30-7]

Am I the only one who thinks Woodward has just admitted that the IPCC can't possibly conclude that more malaria would not accompany global warming - since this would undermine the emissions reduction argument?

A grotesque aspect of the malaria issue is that anyone who truly cares about this disease need not concern themselves with global warming. The World Health Organization says 2,000 children under the age of five die from malaria every single day. When's the last time you heard about that on the six o'clock news?

Since we barely spare a thought for today's victims of this terrible disease how can threatening us with more malaria half a century from now be helpful to anyone's cause?

A world that can't rouse itself to do more about today's malaria victims surely has no business using theoretical, sometime-in-the-future victims as ammunition in the climate debate.

31 – EXTINCTION FICTION

In September 2007, during a presentation at the United Nations headquarters in New York, IPCC chairman Pachauri declared that "20-30% of plant and animal species [are] at risk of extinction" due to global warming. A few months later he used his Nobel lecture to tell the world that failure to prevent climate change "could prove extremely harmful for the human race and for all species that share common space on planet earth."

In February 2008, Pachauri cited the 20-30% figure while addressing a committee of the North Carolina legislature. That November he told an audience at a Zurich university that climate change "will reduce biodiversity" – once again referencing the 20-30% figure. By December he'd taken this message to Poland.

Never tiring of the theme, during 2009 and 2010 Pachauri raised the extinction fear repeatedly. It therefore came as a bit of a shock when I discovered that it is by no means clear how the IPCC arrived at these scary numbers.

In Chapter 4 of the 2007 Working Group 2 report, in a section titled *Global synthesis including impacts on biodiversity*, one paragraph ends with the following:

Based on all above findings and our compilation (Figure 4.4, Table 4.1) **we estimate** that on average 20% to 30% of species assessed are **likely** to be at increasingly high risk of extinction from climate change impacts **possibly** within this century as global mean temperatures exceed 2°C to 3°C relative to pre-industrial levels...**The uncertainties remain large**, however, since for about 2°C temperature increase the percentage **may be** as low as 10% or for about 3°C as high as 40% and, **depending** on biota, the range is between 1% and 80% (Table 4.1; Thomas et al., 2004a; Malcolm et al., 2006). As global average temperature exceeds 4°C above pre-industrial levels, model projections **suggest** significant extinctions (40-70% species assessed) around the globe (Table 4.1).

Please note the words I've bolded. When people talk about *estimates, possibilities, large uncertainties, likelies, maybes,* and *suggestions*; when their guesses range from 10 to 40%, and from 1 to 80% – they aren't saying much of anything. Nevertheless, the IPCC's thinking on this matter does seem to be summed up by this excerpt.

Please also note the two studies that get mentioned by name. One is by Chris Thomas (plus 18 co-authors). The second is by Jay Malcolm (plus four co-authors). According to the IPCC, the Malcolm paper - which discusses vegetation only - estimates that different kinds of ecosystems could lose between 2 and 47% of their current area.

When the public hears about extinction, however, it thinks of animals. The Thomas paper (described as examining both flora and fauna planet wide) estimates that between 9 and 31% of species are "committed to extinction" if the average global temperature rises 1.2 to 2 degrees.

The IPCC lists dozens of other research papers, but those are more limited in scope. One examines Australia's golden bowerbird. Others look at Mexican butterflies, Hawaii's honeycreepers (small birds), and Antarctic snails.

It would appear, therefore, that the IPCC's 20-30% planet-wide extinction estimate rests heavily on the Thomas paper. It is the only research cited by the IPCC that claims to be global and to have considered both animals and plant life.

Incidentally, I'm not the only person who has come to this conclusion. Law professor Jason Johnston raised this matter in his cross-examination of the IPCC.

Cue the dramatic music, because this is where the train leaves the track. What Pachauri's many audiences have had no way of knowing is that the Thomas paper was controversial long before the IPCC decided to accord it center stage in its analysis.

In 2004, *Nature* - a UK science weekly - started off the New Year with a bang. The cover of it's January 8th issue featured a fabulous close-up photo of a lizard. *Feeling the heat. Biodiversity losses due to global warming* declared the headline. Pages 145-148 introduced the Thomas paper to the world, after which the story was picked up by mainstream news outlets. As one scholar later observed: "It is rare for a scientific paper to be the lead item on the evening news, or to fill the front pages of our national newspapers, but the Thomas *et al.* paper received exceptional worldwide media attention."

Many experts, however, consider this paper to be a load of rubbish.

Enter Daniel Botkin. Considered one of the pre-eminent biologists of the 20th century, he helped develop some of the first computer models used by ecologists. And on that point he has a word of warning. Specialists, he says, understand that theoretical models "*should not be taken literally*" (my italics).

In addition to degrees in physics and biology, Botkin has four decades of professional experience under his belt. He has taught at several universities including Yale and the University of California, Santa Barbara – where he was chair of the Environmental Studies program for six years.

Botkin calls the Thomas study "the worst paper I have ever read in a major scientific journal." On his blog he explains:

First, the paper uses a theory that is inappropriate and illogical for the question. Second, the data on which the calculations are based - the areas of the world's biomes - are crude, lacking estimates of measurement error. My textbook *Environmental Science: Earth as a Living Planet* has a chapter on the scientific method in which I state that "a measurement without a statement about its degree of uncertainty is meaningless."

That this was a paper with shortcomings is confirmed by the fact that, by July 2004 (six months after it first appeared), *Nature* had received, edited, and published three separate critiques.

The first one pointed out that, rather than using well-established, universally recognized methods to arrive at its conclusions the Thomas team had employed a novel (and therefore unproven) analytical approach.

The second critique accused the Thomas authors of circular mathematical reasoning and of jumping to conclusions. It said the effects of climate change are difficult to anticipate since the largest number of species actually live in the tropics - and in a warming world, the overall size of that climate zone might well expand.

The third pointed out that because no one yet understands the role genetics plays when species attempt to adapt to changing environments, certain assumptions in the Thomas paper "may not be justified" and certain of its methods may "yield poor results." [note 31-1]

The misgivings about the Thomas paper didn't end there. In July 2005 a conservation biologist at Oxford University had his own paper accepted for publication in a prominent British journal. Owen Lewis devotes 6,000 words to explaining why the findings of the Thomas paper are highly questionable.

He points out that the "widespread ability of species to persist if transplanted or introduced outside their current range" suggests the natural world is more resilient than we might think. (Tomatoes, for example, are native to South America. Introduced to Europe during the 1500s, they thrived to such an extent they became a cornerstone of Italian cuisine.)

The Thomas paper studied only populations known to occupy relatively small geographic ranges. This is a problem, says Lewis, because it is "well known that species with small geographic ranges are particularly prone to extinctions."

Moreover, because so little is known about the tropical invertebrates that constitute "the bulk of global biodiversity" Lewis says scholars "are certainly not in a position to predict" what might happen to them in the future.

The long and short of it? Lewis thinks nothing in the Thomas paper should be extrapolated to the entire globe. The layers upon layers of uncertainty, he says, should "make us very wary."

Soon afterward a scholar at the Helmholtz Centre for Environmental Research in Germany authored yet another paper disputing the Thomas findings. While it's one thing, argued Carsten Dormann, to employ ecological models to generate hypotheses for further testing, it's another matter entirely to present the results of these modeling exercises as predictions that policy makers and the public then interpret as forecasts.

The problems associated with the Thomas approach, he said, are "so numerous and fundamental that common ecological sense should caution us against putting much faith in...their findings."

Finally, by March 2007 a paper by Botkin, the eminent biologist, had also been published. Co-authored with 18 other scholars from the US, Denmark, Spain, the UK, Australia, and Switzerland, this paper accuses many researchers in that field of employing techniques whose reliability has never been confirmed to make predictions about the future. "Of the modeling papers we have reviewed, only a few were validated," they report.

In the opinion of these authors, the Thomas paper "may have greatly overestimated the probability of extinction." Declaring that the past sheds important light on the threat climate change may pose in the future, they noted that:

> the fossil record indicates that, in most regions, surprisingly few species went extinct during the [last 2.5 million years] - in North America, for example, only one tree species is known to have gone extinct...

Serious problems need to be overcome, they said, before "too much weight can be placed" on the methods used in the

Thomas paper. In other words, Botkin and his co-authors made it clear this is not top-notch research.

So once again, a paper on which the IPCC chose to rest its case is highly problematic. By the time the 2007 Climate Bible was released the Thomas paper had already been thoroughly demolished.

In fairness, at the time the IPCC report was being written, its authors may have been genuinely unaware of the Dormann and Botkin responses since they were still in the works. But they would have known about the three critiques published by *Nature*. And, as I've mentioned, the Lewis piece was accepted for publication in July 2005 - well prior to Pachauri's completed-before-January-2006 cutoff. [note 31-2]

So now imagine you are among the 31 individuals assigned to write the chapter of the Climate Bible that deals with species extinction. You know the purpose of the IPCC is to "provide rigorous and balanced scientific information" - just like it says on its website.

Is there any way you can cite the findings of the Thomas paper but not tell your readers about the controversy it generated? Is it honest to neglect to mention that the same journal that published the Thomas paper followed up six months later with not one, not two, but three critiques? Is it scientific to fail to discuss the fact that another harsh appraisal of some 6,000 words in length was authored by a scholar at Oxford?

Yet that is precisely what happened.

So who wrote this IPCC chapter? Its two most senior people are Andreas Fischlin, a biologist from Switzerland, and Guy Midgley, a biologist from South Africa.

Fischlin helped write the 2001 and 2005 editions of the Climate Bible, and is involved in the one currently underway. His academic bio, however, contains something of a bombshell.

It tells us he has long been a member of the Swiss delegation "in all UNFCCC (United Nations Framework Convention on Climate Change) negotiations." In others words, Fischlin is no disinterested scientist. Anyone partaking directly in UN climate negotiations is involved in climate change politicking at the very highest levels.

Would it surprise you to learn that the second leader of this chapter - Guy Midgley - is, in fact, one of the authors of the notorious Thomas paper? (Another Thomas co-author, Lesley Hughes, also worked on this same chapter.)

By now it has become painfully obvious that the IPCC implausibly thinks its personnel are exempt from normal human failings. It chooses to believe that its authors are capable of remaining rigorously objective whenever the merits of their own work are being assessed. A total of 23 papers in which Midgley was involved were cited by this IPCC chapter. The public has no way of knowing how the quality of the other 22 compares to that of the soundly thrashed Thomas paper. [note 31-3]

Midgley has once again been named an author for the upcoming edition of the Climate Bible. It's rather a mystery, though, how his expertise in "plant ecophysiology and stress tolerance" equips him to be one of two senior people for a chapter examining human-centered *Adaptation opportunities, constraints and limitations.*

(If someone were trying to control the overall message in a report like the Climate Bible they might well find it useful to keep re-appointing a core group of trusted individuals to leadership positions - regardless of whether their expertise actually matched.)

Eight more people served as lead authors in the species extinction chapter. American biologist Jeff Price appears first on the list. He holds scientific degrees and teaches at universities. But that doesn't alter the fact that his orientation is overtly activist.

In 2002 he was the director of climate change impact studies for the American Bird Conservancy - an advocacy group. None of the critiques of the Thomas paper may have made it into this chapter's list of references, but a *Birdwatcher's Guide to Global Warming* co-written by Price and published by his employer did. Price has worked for the United Nations Environment Programme and is now employed by yet another activist group, the World Wildlife Fund.

When interviewed in 2007, Price told a reporter: "Many of us *believe* we are on the threshold of a *massive extinction event*" (my italics). But as any detective will tell you, there are opinions and then there are facts.

Revisiting the world's-top-experts question for a moment, there is little indication that Price meets that threshold. Moreover, it's worth noting that others who worked on this chapter include not just Fischlin but two computer modelers whose doctorates were supervised by him. [note 31-4]

To sum up, therefore, we have a chapter that contributed a crucial finding to the 2007 edition of the Climate Bible. The claim that 20-30% of the Earth's species are at risk of extinction has been a hallmark of Pachauri's speeches ever since.

But a look at that chapter reveals it, too, depends almost entirely on a single, highly questionable piece of research. Moreover, a number of that chapter's authors are overtly political actors, suffer from conflict-of-interest, have personal connections to one of its leaders, and don't come close to being world-class experts.

But wait, there's a cherry on top: five out of 10 of this chapter's most senior personnel also have a formal, documented link to the World Wildlife Fund.

Leaders Fischlin and Midgley both belong to the WWF's Climate Witness Scientific Advisory Panel. According to an internal WWF document, the purpose of the Climate Witness initiative is to heighten the public's "sense of urgency" about climate change. Scientists are recruited by the WWF to add a veneer of scientific respectability to anecdotal observations supplied by people who consider themselves a 'Climate Witness.'

Lead authors Rik Leemans and Brij Gopal also belong to this panel. As has already been mentioned, lead author Jeff Price is currently a WWF employee. That makes five WWF-affiliated lead authors. Three additional personnel (who served as contributing authors) are likewise panel members – Antoine Guisan, Christian Körner and Lesley Hughes.

There is no way to know, therefore, which sections of this IPCC chapter represent the opinions of scientists who've jumped into bed with the WWF and which sections are, in fact, scientifically sound.

As chairman Pachauri would say, the species extinction portion of the Climate Bible belongs in the dustbin.

The original version of this chapter ended with the word *dustbin* above. But when this book was fact-checked prior to publication something startling occurred. My fact-checker (who prefers to remain anonymous) observed that the WWF advisory panel included not just the names I've mentioned but many other recognizable individuals. This prompted me to look closely at the panel in its entirety - and to read some of the background material.

What I then discovered would, in a sensible universe, be sufficient to vaporize the IPCC's credibility - now and forever, once and for all. Beginning in 2004 (around the time that work was beginning on the 2007 Climate Bible) the WWF systematically began recruiting IPCC authors. By late 2008 it says it had persuaded 130 "leading climate scientists mostly, but not exclusively, from the Intergovernmental Panel on Climate Change" to join its parallel panel.

Governments around the world tell us that the scientists involved in the IPCC are individuals with impeccable credentials and sound judgment. In fact, large numbers of them suffer from impaired judgment.

These people deliberately chose to link their scientific reputations to a group that believes: "*It is nearly impossible to overstate the threat of climate change.*" They chose to muddy the water by aligning themselves with lobbyists at the same time that they were examining some of the world's most important questions.

Rather than remaining aloof, rather than striving for impartiality (and an appearance of impartiality), they chose to fraternize with the lynch mob outside the jailhouse door - with the folks who have no doubt that a crime has been committed and that the person in custody is the guilty party.

In the footnote that follows, I list 78 IPCC personnel who are also members of the WWF panel. People on this list either played some role in the 2007 Climate Bible or are currently helping to write the next IPCC report which is expected to be completed in 2013 and released in 2014.

147

On this list are 23 coordinating lead authors - those the IPCC placed in charge of an entire chapter. It also includes Osvaldo Canziani. Having served as Working Group 2 co-chair for both the 2001 and 2007 reports, he is one of the IPCC's most senior officials.

After a few days of searching, cross-checking, and tabulating here are my findings with respect to the IPCC's 2007 report:

- 28 out of 44 chapters (two-thirds) included at least one individual affiliated with the WWF
- 100% of the chapters in Working Group 2 – all 20 of them - included at least 1 WWF-affiliated scientist
- 15 out of 44 chapters (one-third) were *led* by WWF-affiliated scientists – their coordinating lead authors belong to the panel
- in three instances, chapters were led by *two* WWF-affiliated coordinating lead authors

Ladies and gentlemen, the IPCC has been infiltrated. It has been wholly and entirely compromised. [note 31-5]

32 – THE HOCKEY STICK

An entire book has been written about yet another scandalous IPCC episode. One cannot read the gripping tale told in Andrew Montford's *The Hockey Stick Illusion* and come away feeling that all is well in the world of climate science.

In brief, the 'hockey stick' is the nickname given to a temperature graph that became the central icon of the 2001 edition of the Climate Bible. It purported to show that temperature had been roughly stable from the year 1000 AD until the 20th century - after which it began to shoot up dramatically. The flattish part of the line reminded people of the long handle of an ice-hockey stick at rest, while the uptick resembled the blade.

Different versions of this graph appeared in five separate places in the 2001 Climate Bible. When the co-chair of Working Group 1 presented the IPCC's findings to the media, an enlarged version of the graph was displayed behind him. Since then, it has appeared in a variety of government documents and featured prominently in the documentary film version of Al Gore's *An Inconvenient Truth.* [note 32-1]

Depending on whether you're talking to a climate skeptic or a climate activist (people in the second camp control the Wikipedia pages on this and many other topics related to global warming), the hockey stick graph has either been totally discredited or remains a sound piece of science whose findings have been confirmed by several independent studies. [note 32-2] As Montford's book explains, such claims of independent corroboration are suspect, since these studies were conducted by many of the same small clique of researchers, use similarly flawed statistical techniques, and/or rely on the same dubious sources of data.

For the purposes of this discussion the important point is that the IPCC performed no due diligence before according the hockey stick graph such prominence. It didn't bother to check the math.

It's important to appreciate that this graph presented a totally new view of the temperature record than the one long accepted by scholars. The IPCC itself had included a more traditional temperature graph in its 1990 Climate Bible. It showed a warm period during the Middle Ages - represented by an upward bump in the temperature line. This was followed by a period known as the Little Ice Age, which ended around 1850 - represented by a somewhat longer downward dip in the line. [note 32-3]

It is both peculiar and ironic that an organization that so vigorously claims to represent a worldwide scientific consensus has systematically 'disappeared' so many consensus views held by so many different kinds of researchers. The IPCC ignores the consensus among hurricane experts that there is no discernible link to global warning. It ignores the consensus among those who study natural disasters that there is no relationship between human greenhouse gas emissions and the rising cost of these disasters. It ignores the consensus among *bona fide* malaria experts that global warming has not caused malaria to spread.

In each case the IPCC substitutes its own version of reality. In each case that version of reality makes global warming appear more frightening than genuine experts believe the available evidence indicates.

The hockey stick graph is another example of this phenomenon. Don Easterbrook has studied and taught geology for the past 50 years. He is the author of three textbooks and 150 research papers. He says that when geologists first saw the hockey stick graph, most of them laughed:

If you look in GeoRef, which is the bibliography for publications in geology, you will find 485 papers on the Medieval Warm Period and you'll find 1,413 on the Little Ice Age. So the total number of papers in the geologic literature is 1,900. And we're expected to believe that one curve [based on] tree rings is going to overturn all of those 1,900 papers? I don't think so. [note 32-4]

Geophysicist David Deming has expressed similar concerns. The Medieval Warm Period, he says has "been recognized in the scientific literature for decades." In one fell swoop, however, the authors of the papers that produced the hockey stick graph made it vanish. "Normally in science," says Deming "when you have a novel result that appears to overturn pre-vious work, you have to demonstrate why the earlier work was wrong." But the IPCC didn't ask the hockey stick authors to do so before it embraced their findings.

The lead author for the pair of papers that produced the hockey stick graph was an American geophysicist named Michael Mann. He received his PhD in 1998 and in April of that year his first hockey stick paper was published by *Nature*. The second appeared in a different journal the following March.

In what is now a familiar refrain, the fact that Mann had only just acquired his PhD was no barrier to the IPCC recruiting him, in the late 1990s, to be one of its lead authors. In the blink of an eye Mann was transformed into one of the world's top experts. Equally disturbing is that the IPCC assigned him to help write the very chapter of the Climate Bible that subsequently decided his graph was superior to all other temperature reconstructions.

Mathematician Steve McIntyre's curiosity was piqued after the hockey stick graph began appearing in news reports and was cited in government-produced literature distributed to Canadian homes. [note 32-5] When he attempted, in early 2003, to examine the calculations that produced the graph he discovered some disturbing things.

Mann's data wasn't publicly archived on a website run by the journals that had published his findings. Instead, McIntyre was obliged to contact Mann directly. A file was eventually sent to him, but the numbers didn't add up. Attempting to puzzle out why this should be the case, McIntyre discovered a number of irregularities, including labeling errors and the use of obsolete data.

McIntyre teamed up with a fellow Canadian, economist Ross McKitrick. By October, they'd jointly published a paper that showed that once the errors found in Mann's work were corrected the hockey-stick-shaped line disappeared. [note 32-6]

Mann responded by claiming that McIntyre had been using the wrong data. Rather than sending a new file, he provided the two Canadians with the address of an online archive. They examined this archive and, in McKitrick's words, discovered that the data there "corresponded almost exactly to the file we had originally been working with. However it differed in important ways" from how Mann had described it in the paper that had appeared in *Nature*.

When these discrepancies were pointed out, Mann replied that the Canadians had failed to exactly replicate his computational steps. Recalls McKitrick: "So we requested his computational code to eliminate these easily-resolved differences. To our surprise he refused to supply his computer code."

Remember, the hockey stick graph was the most important piece of visual information in the 2001 Climate Bible. The public was told by governments around the world that this graph proved something alarming was going on, that temperatures in the 20th century were the highest in 1,000 years. In McKitrick's view, without this graph it's unlikely there would have been a Kyoto Protocol. [note 32-7]

So what happened when an attempt was made to verify its accuracy? The lead scientist, who is employed at a publicly-funded university and who uses public dollars to carry out his research, declared the computer code to be his own private property. Really.

In 2005 Mann sent a letter to the head of a subcommittee of the US Congress investigating this matter. It declared:

It also bears emphasis that my computer program is a private piece of intellectual property...whether I make my computer programs publicly available or not is a decision that is mine alone to make...

Earlier in this book I quoted a professor from Stanford University named Jon Claerbout. He's the person who says that: "An article about computational science in a scientific publication isn't the scholarship itself, it's merely advertising...The actual scholarship is the complete software development environment and *the complete set of instructions which generated the figures*" (my italics). [note 32-8] This is because lines of computer code may contain small mistakes that have big consequences.

Mann, on the other hand, is of the opinion that his computer instructions are his to hoard if he wants to. Thus, he arrogantly informed the chairman of the congressional subcommittee that it was a false premise that his computer code was necessary to reproduce his results. To support his position, Mann quoted a snooty 2003 e-mail from David Verardo, a senior employee at the National Science Foundation, sent to McIntyre:

> Dr. Mann and his other US colleagues are under no obligation to provide you with any additional data beyond the extensive data sets they have already made available. He is not required to provide you with computer programs, codes, etc. His research is published in the peer-reviewed literature which has passed muster with the editors of those journals and other scientists who have reviewed his manuscripts. You are free to [conduct] your analysis of climate data and he is free to [conduct] his. The passing of time and evolving new knowledge about Earth's climate will eventually tell the full story of changing climate. I would expect that you would respect the views of the US NSF on the issue of data access and intellectual property for US investigators as articulated by me to you in my last message under the advisement of the US NSF's Office of General Counsel.

Please note that last sentence. The Office of General Counsel is the legal department. Michael Mann and the National Science Foundation are hiding behind lawyers.

According to climate change activists it's only the future of the planet that is at stake. But rather than share his computer code so that his calculations might be verified, Mann chose to lawyer-up. Yeah, that's how a real scientist behaves. I'm sure Einstein did that all the time.

There is, of course, a bigger problem - and that's that Mann's anti-scientific behavior has been aided and abetted by the American science establishment. Let us have no illusions about what happened here. The National Science Foundation, a major funder of scientific research, didn't defend transparency. It didn't acknowledge the iconic status of Mann's graph. It betrayed not the slightest awareness that this is an unusual and exceptional situation. Instead, it talked airily about peer review and the passage of time. And then it told McIntyre to piss off.

Has Mann become a pariah in scientific or academic circles as a result of his refusal to reveal the computer code connected to one of the most important graphs in history? You be the judge.

In April 2011, he was a guest speaker for two nights in a row at the University of Nebraska-Lincoln. [note 32-9] According to an announcement by that university, Mann is "one of the country's leading climate scientists." He is "the director of the Penn State Earth System Science Center." Moreover, he "has been organizing committee chair for the National Academy of Sciences 'Frontiers of Science.'"

Oh, and his speaking gig was "supported by a Distinguished Lecturer Grant."

There is far more to the hockey stick story, and much of it is equally appalling. For example, eminent statisticians who've examined the process by which Mann arrived at his conclusions say it includes statistical errors. They've observed that while climatologists such as Mann rely heavily on statistical analyses there's no evidence they make any effort to work with people who have statistical training. [note 32-10]

The essential point here is that the IPCC aggressively promoted a graph that had been produced by a young scientist who'd just been awarded his PhD. Even though that graph overturned decades of scholarship, even though it negated a widespread consensus about what the temperature record of the past 1,000 years looked like, the IPCC didn't bother to verify its accuracy. What has been described as "one of the most rigorous scientific review bodies in existence" felt no need to ensure that its case wasn't being built on quicksand.

Nor has it intervened since then, prevailing on Mann to do the right thing - to come clean so that doubts may be put to rest and matters clarified once and for all.

In the 2007 version of the Climate Bible the IPCC discreetly backed away from the hockey stick graph. But it hasn't issued a correction. Nor has it explained or defended the underlying calculations on which the graph is based.

Is this really how people who think our climate is on the verge of a dangerous tipping point would behave?

33 – PEER REVIEW IPCC-STYLE

We've encountered the IPCC's internal review process a few times already, but it's worth shining a spotlight directly on this process since IPCC officials boast about it often and journalists can't stop praising it.

The Climate Bible is, indeed, written by hundreds of people. If 30 individuals, say, are connected to each chapter and there are 44 chapters, that adds up to 1,300 authors - give or take since, as we've seen, those who belong to the Insiders' Club frequently participate in more than one chapter.

The IPCC says that, *additionally*, there were 2,500 expert reviewers involved with the 2007 Climate Bible, spread across three Working Groups. That number is impressive but it's also an exaggeration. Since IPCC authors often also serve as expert reviewers many of them were counted twice.

An early draft of the Climate Bible was submitted to these expert reviewers for comment. Based on their remarks another draft was prepared and again shown to the reviewers. It's implied that all of this - the vast number of people involved and the double-round of feedback - helps make this document rock solid. Not only is this report written by hundreds of scientists, we're told, thousands more read the early drafts. The overt implication is that the IPCC's conclusions can therefore be trusted.

When IPCC author and meteorologist Richard Somerville provided written testimony to a US Congress sub-committee in March 2011, he said that "the multiple stages of peer review" to which IPCC reports are subjected is one of the reasons lawmakers can have faith in these documents.

Robert Watson, who served as chairman of the IPCC between 1997 and 2002, advised readers in an article published in 2010 that IPCC reports "undergo two rounds of peer review."

According to the World Wildlife Fund, the Climate Bible represents "the biggest and most profound peer-review process of scientific findings of all time."

In 2007 we were assured, by a journalist working for the *Los Angeles Times*, that the IPCC is considered "the preeminent authority on climate change" because of "its meticulous, peer-reviewed process."

In 2004, science commentator Chris Mooney dismissed climate skeptic arguments by pointing to the IPCC's "highly rigorous global peer review process."

But what takes place at the IPCC is a far cry from what is normally understood by the term *peer review* - and concern that this is an inappropriate and misleading description is not new. Back in 2002, Sonja Boehmer-Christiansen and Aynsley Kellow raised this issue in their book about the Kyoto Protocol. They observed that while "IPCC leaders lay claim to the use of peer review in the production of IPCC reports" what occurs there "falls short of the usual standards of peer review" in "five important ways."

Traditionally, they point out, peer review is anonymous. Reviewers can speak freely because their identities remain unknown. The IPCC, however, attaches names to each comment before these comments are shown to its authors. This practically invites authors to dismiss some remarks outright - either because they think the person making them isn't important, or because they consider the person to be a climate skeptic who shouldn't be paid any mind.

Before sending a paper out for review a journal will remove the author's name. This helps ensure the paper is judged on its own merits. Whether the author is an obscure researcher in the field or a minor celebrity shouldn't color a reviewer's evaluation. At the IPCC, however, the identity of a chapter's most senior authors is known to everyone. Since some of those authors wield considerable influence in their field, lesser personages may be reluctant to challenge or offend them when acting as IPCC expert reviewers.

An equally serious issue is that, when peer review happens in academia, the journal is a neutral party. The author submits a paper, the reviewers submit their comments, and the editor takes both into consideration before deciding whether the paper should be published, rewritten, or rejected. The editor is the one with the power, since he or she determines whose point-of-view should prevail.

In the case of the IPCC, there are no neutral parties - no umpires at the baseball game. The process is stacked in favor of the authors - who themselves decide whether they've scored a home run or have won the tournament. Expert reviewers may think the authors have struck out, but there's no umpire they can appeal to who will listen to both sides and then make an independent ruling.

(In fact, it is only much later, after the Climate Bible has been finalized and released, that the reviewers get to see how the authors replied to their concerns. Oddly, while the IPCC ensures that expert reviewers are identified, its authors are permitted to respond anonymously. No one is apparently concerned that this double-standard encourages authors to be dismissive, since they run no risk of being called to account after the fact.)

The differences don't end there. In a journal setting, peer reviewers read the entire article under consideration. At the IPCC, expert reviewers examine and comment on whatever strikes their fancy out of a report that totals 3,000 pages. Because reviewers aren't assigned to specific sections, many parts of the Climate Bible may receive no external scrutiny whatsoever.

Furthermore, as Boehmer-Christiansen and Kellow pointed out a decade ago, "there is no possibility that the draft chapter will *not* be published" (their italics). This means that the worst, most dreaded outcome associated with the academic peer review process - that a paper will be rejected outright - is completely absent. [note 33-1]

What goes on at the IPCC is not peer review as that term is normally understood. It's far closer to what occurred when I wrote this book. At a certain juncture, I e-mailed a draft to colleagues, friends, and relatives. Those people generously took time out of their busy lives to read my manuscript and to make suggestions about how it might be improved. The onus was on me to have the good sense to adopt these suggestions.

There was no anonymity. There was no neutral party telling me if I didn't make the suggested changes my book couldn't proceed. There was no risk that, based on opinions expressed by these people, my book would be stopped dead in its tracks.

Inviting outsiders to make *suggestions* is not the same thing as academic peer review. Not by a long shot. That the IPCC has long equated its informal process with the far more rigorous, independent, high-stakes process people think of when they hear the term *peer review* is disturbing.

Can the individuals quoted above really, truly not tell the difference between academic peer review and what goes on at the IPCC? Or are they trying to pull a fast one?

Without a doubt, the IPCC's more relaxed review process undermines the quality of its reports. We've encountered at least five examples of this:

First, we saw how the IPCC discourages its expert reviewers from looking too closely at the underlying data on which research papers rely. By attempting to examine this sort of data Steve McIntyre attracted the ire of a senior IPCC official who threatened to strike him from the reviewers list.

Second, despite objections from an expert reviewer, we discovered that the 2007 Climate Bible relied on press releases as a source of information.

Third, although the IPCC laudably heeded criticism expressed by expert reviewers about a damages-from-natural-disasters graph, its response was to substitute a new, mystery graph that was arguably even worse. At a journal, after the new graph had been produced, the editor would have shown it to the reviewers. At the IPCC, once the two rounds of review have been completed, that's it. Changes made by IPCC authors after that point receive no oversight.

Which brings us to the fourth example - the fact that 26 references to the Stern Review were added to 12 different IPCC chapters after the work of the expert reviewers had already been completed. IPCC expert reviewers were blissfully unaware of the 26 ways the Stern Review was being used to support arguments in the Climate Bible and so could not have objected.

The fifth example is from the *This is Called Cheating* chapter. It concerns the May 2007 issue of *Climatic Change* that contains 16 papers cited by the Climate Bible as evidence. Only one of these had been accepted for publication early enough that expert reviewers would have been able to examine it. Since they had no knowledge of the others, it cannot be said that the use of those papers had the blessing of the IPCC's expert reviewers.

But there is another spectacular demonstration of the IPCC's lax review process in action. In early 2010 it attracted rather a lot of media attention.

On January 17, the London *Sunday Times* ran a story under the headline *World misled over Himalayan glacier meltdown*. It said the 2007 Climate Bible had claimed that Himalayan glaciers could vanish by 2035 as a result of climate change. The IPCC had cited a single source of evidence for this prediction - a document prepared by the World Wildlife Fund. In turn, the WWF had cited a magazine - the *New Scientist*. The magazine, for its part, said its information came from an interview with a single glacier expert, Syed Iqbal Hasnain.

According to the *Sunday Times*, Hasnain was "a little-known Indian scientist" who had since admitted he'd pulled the number out of the air. It wasn't, he conceded, based on any formal research. Other glacier experts, the newspaper reported, considered the 2035 estimate "inherently ludicrous." The director of a polar research institute was quoted as saying a complete meltdown within 25 years was "unrealistically high." Canadian geography professor, Graham Cogley, who'd "long been unhappy with the IPCC's finding" was credited with helping to bring the mistake to the world's attention.

(Incidentally, a mere six weeks earlier America's *Time* magazine had built an entire feature article around Hasnain. He was quoted on that occasion in full political-activist mode, declaring: "The debate is over. We know the science. We see the threat. The time for action is now.")

The newspaper further reported that one of the leaders of the IPCC chapter that contained the Himalayan glacier error had been contacted. His name was Murari Lal and it so happens he served in three other capacities for the 2007 Climate Bible. The paragraph about him in the *Times* is important for what it says about how the IPCC operates:

> Lal himself admits he knows little about glaciers. "I am not an expert on glaciers and I have not visited the region so I have to rely on credible published research. The comments in the WWF report were made by a respected Indian scientist and it was reasonable to assume he knew what he was talking about," he said.

Comments appearing in an activist publication were *assumed* to be correct. That's all these IPCC authors required.

The *Sunday Times* coverage was only the beginning. Although media interest in North America was grudging, in the UK and India this was a big story. As a direct result, the InterAcademy Council (IAC) established the committee that subsequently sponsored the online questionnaire I've discussed throughout this book. The committee's mandate was to take a close look at the IPCC's policies and procedures.

Nothing like this had ever happened before. For more than 20 years, this spoiled child of an organization had been left entirely to its own devices. The world had simply accepted, at face value, its rosy view of itself.

The committee was pressed for time and therefore limited in its scope. Within the space of four months its members listened to live presentations, collected responses via an online questionnaire, deliberated amongst themselves, and then produced a 100+ page report. This report made it clear the IPCC's review process is dysfunctional.

The embarrassing glacier error, it said, could have been entirely avoided had the IPCC merely listened to its own expert reviewers. One of them had observed that its Himalaya section was internally inconsistent. Another drew the IPCC's attention to peer-reviewed research that contained more cautious conclusions about the rate at which the glaciers are melting.

Mistakes had been noticed. They had been pointed out. But in the words of the committee, the IPCC "did not change the text."

The committee said "significant improvements" were necessary. Even with such improvements, however, it acknowledged that the IPCC's review process would still not be "truly independent." This is because the responsibility for responding to reviewer comments rests solely with people who are affiliated with the IPCC.

True independence, said the committee, would only be possible if personnel unconnected to the IPCC served as neutral umpires. It is not clear, said the committee, "what scientific body has the recognized legitimacy and capacity to carry out such a large task". [note 33-2]

To sum up, therefore, the IPCC is inordinately proud of its review process. It expects us to be impressed by how many people are involved and by how many comments it receives and addresses.

But this process is fatally flawed. It is not independent. It is easily short-circuited and circumvented. Nothing about it measures up to academic peer review.

Those who have been promulgating the myth that what the IPCC does is equivalent to academic peer review should be ashamed of themselves.

34 – A DAMNING ASSESSMENT

After the InterAcademy Council's report was released in August 2010, I wrote a blog post in which I described that moment as a turning point. The committee hadn't addressed every concern about the IPCC, but it had accomplished one task admirably: it had knocked the IPCC off its pedestal At last, science academies were beginning to act like grown ups in relation to this delinquent child.

The committee's report blows smoking holes through just about everything chairman Rajendra Pachauri has told us about his organization.

Transparency, it said, is not one of the IPCC's strengths.

Although procedures were in place regarding the flagging of non-peer-reviewed literature, in droll understatement the committee said it was "clear that these procedures are not always followed."

Observing that the IPCC frequently claims to have high confidence in "statements for which there is little evidence," the committee blamed this partly on the fact that still other IPCC procedures aren't adhered to. It therefore found itself in the awkward position of advocating additional policies while at the same time acknowledging that the ones already in existence aren't being enforced.

As for the chairman himself, the committee suggested ever-so-diplomatically that Pachauri should step down. No one, it said, should serve more than a single term. A "12-year appointment (two terms) is too long for a field as dynamic and contested as climate change." Having assumed the helm of the IPCC in 2002, Pachauri is well into his second term.

Overall, the committee found "significant shortcomings in each major step of IPCC's assessment process." Let me repeat that: The first time an independent group of people took a close look at the way the IPCC conducts its affairs, those people concluded that *each step* in the IPCC assessment process suffers from *significant shortcomings*. [note 34-1]

The contrast between the professional tone of the report and Pachauri's cavalier approach was most apparent with regard to the question of conflict-of-interest.

In a 2010 interview with *The Economist* magazine Pachauri was asked: "Isn't it rather remarkable that you should have this [important and influential] organisation that does not have any procedure for dealing with conflict of interest?"

Pachauri indolently responded that "if the governments who govern the IPCC determine that there should be something of this nature" he was sure it would be put in place.

When pressed on the fact that he himself had done nothing in this regard despite being in charge for eight years he replied: "Why would I raise something, unless there is a reason for me to raise it?" He had never, he said, "felt the need for it" since his own behavior was "above reproach."

The committee, however, was adamant. It said the IPCC should "adopt a rigorous conflict of interest policy that applies to all individuals directly involved in the preparation of IPCC reports."

Perhaps because of time constraints, the committee didn't investigate complaints that IPCC personnel routinely pass judgment on their own work (as well on the work of their academic rivals). But it did say the IPCC should "pay special attention to issues of independence and bias to maintain the integrity of, and public confidence in, its results." [note 34-2]

As I write this the first anniversary of the IAC's report is mere weeks away. How much progress has been made? To what degree has the behavior of this delinquent child improved?

Although the committee offered Pachauri a face-saving exit, he declined to take advantage of it. This 71-year-old appears supremely untroubled by the fact that his continued presence undermines the IPCC's credibility. Remaining in the limelight until 2014 is apparently more important to him than the reputation of the organization he leads.

The IPCC receives the bulk of its financial support from a small group of countries. Currently these include Germany, Japan, Switzerland, and the US. Had representatives of those countries joined forces they surely could have pressured Pachauri to step down. But despite the devastating tenor of the IAC report, they chose not to.

(There is, incidentally, an alternative interpretation. The report was delivered at the end of August 2010. In October the IPCC held a previously scheduled plenary meeting in Busan, South Korea. According to an account published in an Indian newspaper, attempting to remove Pachauri at that meeting might have had international political repercussions. "Insiders," reported the newspaper, "said there was a fear that targeting Pachauri could provoke a confrontation between the IPCC's rich and poor member countries." In other words, don't expect the IPCC's leadership to be held to a high standard any time soon. At the end of the day, the IPCC is merely one consideration among many in an international poker game.)

So not only does the damaged-goods chairman remain, but the committee's clear recommendation that the IPCC should strengthen its flagging-of-non-peer-reviewed-material policy has been outrageously flouted. Deciding the flagging rule was too much of a bother, IPCC bureaucrats made it disappear.

As for conflict-of-interest, the IPCC has, at long last, begun to have a conversation about this matter. But please note that, by announcing its new slate of authors nine weeks prior to the release of the IAC committee's report, the IPCC all but ensured that the next edition of the Climate Bible would be exempt.

In May 2011 the IPCC adopted a conflict-of-interest policy, but parts of it remain murky and it's far from clear how the IPCC intends to enforce it. [note 34-3] In June 2011, Pachauri confirmed that this policy doesn't apply to the authors currently working on the upcoming Climate Bible. His reasoning, as he explained it to a newsmagazine, has to be heard to be believed:

> Of course if you look at conflict of interest with respect to authors who are there in the 5th Assessment Report we've already selected them and therefore **it wouldn't be fair** to impose anything that sort of applies retrospectively. [bold added]

With the wellbeing of our children and grandchildren supposedly hanging in the balance, the IPCC's primary concern is whether its authors feel they are being treated fairly. Even now, Pachauri remains oblivious to the real issue: If people no longer regard IPCC reports as neutral, unbiased, and objective there's no point in writing them.

So that's three strikes. Pachauri lingers, the flagging rule has vanished, and real action on conflict-of-interest has been pushed well into the future. It's difficult to see how the IAC's report has improved matters.

But, wait, there's one last point to consider. Observing that the IPCC structure didn't lend itself to responding in a timely fashion when concerns are raised by the media, the committee suggested a new body be established to deal with IPCC business between the scheduled meetings of that organization. It therefore included the following as one of its recommendations:

> The IPCC should establish an Executive Committee to act on its behalf between Plenary sessions. The membership of the Committee should include the IPCC Chair, the Working Group Co-chairs, the senior member of the Secretariat, and **three independent members who include individuals from outside of the climate community**. [bold added] [note 34-4]

In June 2011 Steve McIntyre reported on his blog that the IPCC has, indeed, established this new committee. There's just one problem. While the IAC report said it should contain *three independent* voices, including people from *outside the climate community*, the IPCC thumbed its nose at that advice. In lieu of independent individuals the IPCC instead gave four of its fulltime staff members seats at the table. [note 34-5]

The writers of the IAC report believed the IPCC would benefit from an outside perspective. But the IPCC is having none of it.

35 – IF THE JURY HAS BEEN RIGGED...

In the wake of the high-profile Himalayan glacier scandal, many IPCC-affiliated scientists have attempted to shrug off the incident. OK, they admit, the IPCC review process isn't as airtight as everyone thought. Mistakes happen, no big deal. What's one error in a report 3,000 pages long? [note 35-1]

Their overarching message has been that this doesn't touch the science, that the basic premise that human beings are altering the climate in dangerous ways remains unchallenged. [note 35-2]

I don't know whether to laugh or cry when I hear this argument. What it conveniently ignores is that we've been told for years that *the reason* we should believe in human-caused climate change is because an elaborate and reliable IPCC process had examined matters and pronounced it a genuine and pressing problem.

In 2008, while delivering a speech in California that may be viewed on YouTube, Rajendra Pachauri declared:

The point is you have a transparent, comprehensive, extremely widespread process involving the best scientists and experts from all over the world *telling you that climate change is for real*. [italics added]

A year earlier he'd insisted that the strengths of the IPCC's process were "valid reasons to accept the science" of global warming.

In 2007 Penny Wong, who later became Australia's climate change minister, wrote a newspaper opinion piece in which she declared there was "overwhelming scientific evidence" of human-caused climate change and that questioning this "was nothing short of dangerous."

For proof she pointed to that year's IPCC report. "These are not," she said, "findings made by one or two scientists " In her words, they are "findings resulting from the meticulous research, and rigorous peer assessment, of hundreds of scientists around the globe under the auspices of an organisation established" by two UN bodies.

That same year American law professor Daniel A. Farber asked in a scholarly paper: "how sure can we be that climate change is a genuine threat? The most reliable source is the IPCC's 2007 report." That report, he said, "is the result of an exhaustive review process" and an "intensive, international scientific effort."

We've been told there is a direct connection between the IPCC's *process* and how much faith we should have in the big-picture conclusion that human-generated greenhouse gases are interfering with the climate. We've been urged to believe in the end result because the IPCC's *process* is itself trustworthy.

If it turns out this process is as full of holes as my colander, scientists and politicians cannot now argue that those holes don't matter.

In a criminal trial we all understand that if the jury has been rigged, the judge has been bought, or the prosecutor has cheated the verdict must be thrown out. It is worthless.

Moreover, improper behavior on the part of only one jury member is sufficient to invalidate a jury's decision. In the case of the IPCC we know that dozens of participants have ties to activist groups with political agendas. We know the health chapter was stacked with public health crusaders. We know neutral parties have never been asked to evaluate the strengths and weakness of climate models - instead the IPCC invites climate modelers to tell us how beautiful their own babies are.

We know the chief justice himself - chairman Rajendra Pachauri - sees climate change action as part of a larger cause. We know that nothing he says about his own organization should be taken at face value - in fact, it's probably dead wrong.

What does all of this tell us?

It says the IPCC process is broken. It says the verdict that humans are responsible for causing dangerous climate change cannot stand.

A new trial must be held.

36 – DISBAND THE IPCC

Large numbers of people believe human-generated carbon dioxide is interfering with our climate. But the truth of the matter is far from clear. When irregularities occur in a criminal trial we all recognize that it's impossible to declare the accused guilty - or innocent.

A new hearing must be convened, and it's vitally important that almost everyone who participated in the previous trial be excluded. The case must be examined anew - with a brand new judge, a brand new jury, and a brand new prosecutor. This fresh, untainted group of people must start from scratch.

The IPCC is currently working on its fifth edition of the Climate Bible. Commonly referred to as AR5 (which stands for *Assessment Report #5*), it is not being written by a fresh set of faces. Quite the opposite.

Pachauri, who authors forewords for Greenpeace publications, is still in charge. This fact, in itself, delivers a fatal blow to AR5's credibility.

Ove Hoegh-Guldberg - whose ties to Greenpeace extend back 17 years - is now leading a chapter. So is Michael Oppenheimer, who worked for the Environmental Defense Fund for more than two decades.

Greenpeace 'legend' Bill Hare is serving as a lead author. Richard Moss, the former World Wildlife Fund vice-president, and Jennifer Morgan, the former WWF chief spokesperson, are both involved.

Andreas Fischlin and Guy Midgley, the two WWF-linked individuals who led the species extinction chapter are participating. So are Rik Leemans and Lesley Hughes, two more WWF-linked individuals from that chapter.

Sari Kovats, who only earned her PhD last year, is leading a chapter. As is Jens Hesselbjerg Christensen - who cited 10 research papers that hadn't even been accepted by a journal when he led an IPCC chapter the last time.

Gabriele Hegerl, who refused outright to allow Steve McIntyre to check her data, is involved. So is Kevin Trenberth - whose hurricane pronouncements sparked Chris Landsea's resignation. Alistair Woodward is now in charge of the health chapter, despite the overtly political treatises he has authored.

And let us not forget Thomas Stocker, the climate modeler who heads AR5's 'hard science' working group. Since he thinks gasoline prices should triple and that everyone should participate in the *grand goal* of de-carbonizing society it's clear his mind is already made up. Do we really suppose that a working group led by him is going to acquit the accused? [note 36-1]

Given the involvement of the above individuals, the findings of the upcoming Climate Bible are already discredited. The refusal of the IPCC to enforce its new conflict-of-interest policy underscores this fact. If significant concerns did not exist there'd be no reason not to apply it now. AR5 is, therefore, thoroughly compromised.

For years we've been told the IPCC is a reputable and professional organization - a grownup in a pinstripe suit. In reality, it's a rule-breaking, not-to-be-trusted, delinquent teenager.

Surely climate activists and climate skeptics can agree on this one thing: the future of the planet is too important to be left in hands such as these. Governments should suspend funding immediately. The IPCC must be disbanded.

Those involved should be sent to bed without any supper. They should also receive a severe tongue lashing.

Many of these people genuinely believe the planet is at risk from human-caused climate change. At the very least they have all been writing reports that can be expected to influence trillions of dollars in expenditures - trillions that won't be available to address other problems. Considering how much is at stake, their behavior has been scandalously unprofessional. What were they thinking?

As for the bigger picture, there's plenty of blame to go around. Lots of grownups had a hand in raising this delinquent teen.

Those who set up the IPCC should have included genuine checks-and-balances from the beginning. The media should have subjected the IPCC to the same kind of scrutiny that helps keep other organizations honest. Environmentalists should have stayed away for everyone's sake.

And scientists - well, my respect for scientists and scientific organizations has plummeted since I began researching this book.

The real moral of this story is that scientists are merely human. They can be as short-sighted and as political and as dishonorable as the rest of us.

~fini~

ABOUT THE AUTHOR

I worked as a journalist during the 1990s, frequently writing difficult, investigative pieces for Canadian magazines and newspapers. Among the editors to whom I reported I had a reputation for tenacity and meticulous documentation.

For four years I wrote a weekly opinion column for *The Toronto Star* - the nation's largest circulation newspaper. Between 1998 and 2001, I was a staffer with the *National Post* - where I wrote feature articles, columns, and served on the editorial board.

In late 2001 the newspaper was sold and more than 100 of us were laid off. I left journalism and ceased writing altogether. I never expected to author another book (my first, published in 1996, was about the women's movement).

By early 2009, however, emotionally-laden climate change coverage was everywhere - including the pages of my most trusted news sources. Much of the analysis struck me as shallow. I began conducting my own research - eventually reading dozens of books that explored multiple sides of the climate debate.

When I learned there are many reputable scientists who don't think global warming is a catastrophe-in-the-making, I was offended that I hadn't heard about them before. I started a website called NOconsensus.org – which was aimed at letting people know there was another side to the story.

For the record, I didn't arrive at my conclusions via FOX News or talk radio. I'm a print-oriented Canadian. I rarely listen to the radio and, other than the occasional hockey game and Obama's inauguration, haven't watched live TV in years. Indeed, I don't recall having ever seen a FOX News broadcast. Right-wing media sources are not, therefore, remotely responsible for my climate change views.

What are those views? After more than two years of research, I'm firmly in the climate skeptic camp. After all journalists are supposed to be skeptical. They aren't supposed to take anyone's word for anything. They're supposed to dig, and question, and challenge.

When I worked as a journalist I was besieged by people who tried to enlist me in their private little wars, who hoped I'd give their side of the story - and only their side of the story - publicity. In my view journalists who allow themselves to be used by climate activists betray their calling - and the public's trust.

I'm also a former vice president of the Canadian Civil Liberties Association (1998-2001). I believe fervently in free speech. That some climate activists have been trying to 'disappear' alternative points-of-view is, therefore, a huge red flag. It's one thing to disagree with people. It's another matter altogether to pretend their opinions don't exist - or to argue that their opinions don't deserve a hearing.

I agree with the American writer, Archibald MacLeish, who declared: "Once you permit those who are convinced of their own superior rightness to censor and silence and suppress those who hold contrary opinions, just at that moment the citadel has been surrendered."

I also agree with John Stuart Mill, who pointed out 150 years ago that censorship harms not just the person whose voice is silenced, but the wider community - since everyone else is denied the right to hear the alternative point-of-view and to make up their own minds. As Mill said, no matter how strongly someone feels, they "have no authority to decide the question for all mankind."

I began a blog called NoFrakkingConsensus – the title of which reveals my growing sense of exasperation. People like Al Gore were trying to shut down the discussion by saying "the debate is over." UN representatives were declaring it *immoral* to even *question* the need for climate change action. They were saying that failing to take such action was *criminally irresponsible*. To me, these were all signs that something was amiss.

In my youth I wore an activist button that read: *Question Authority*. As a feminist who holds an undergraduate degree in women's studies, I believe in making my own decisions. I don't allow myself to be bossed around. Not by men - and not by green activists.

Nor was I born yesterday. By now I've seen too many media-hyped scare stories that didn't pan out. The Y2K Millennium Bug is only one example. We were told January 1st 2000 would be the day the world shut down, that large numbers of businesses would fail, that millions in the third world could starve to death, that Asia would be 'toast'. We were advised that the only people who weren't terrified were those who didn't appreciate the magnitude of the problem. But in the end, it was a non-event.

When I was a child, we were told that forests were being wiped-out by acid rain. This, too, was an overblown non-crisis. Adults sat us down in school and showed us frightening films that, with the passage of time, turned out to be nonsense.

People who want me to believe there's a planetary emergency need to persuade me. I'm not going to take their word for it. If they attempt to browbeat me rather than explaining their position in a calm, rational, and professional manner, I'm not likely to be won over.

The global warming debate is a strange one. I can't think of any other topic in which people go around declaring that 'the debate is over.' Where - and when, precisely - did this *bona fide* debate take place? How was the winner decided? Who made that call - and on what grounds?

It is peculiar, indeed, that people who see things differently try to link my climate views to racists, Holocaust deniers, child murderers, mental illness, and the tobacco industry. It is bizarre that Prime Ministers and other officials think it remotely appropriate to publicly denounce climate skeptics as cowards, saboteurs, and anti-science Flat-Earthers.

In which universe is it sensible to demean and bully those who have reached conclusions that differ from your own? Whatever happened to tolerance and mutual respect?

I spent a few years writing about family law. When it comes to divorce court, it's a given that everyone despises everyone else. There, as in this debate, all the name-calling and maligning of other people's motives is an irrelevant distraction. My job as a journalist is to see past the emotion, to examine the evidence that exists in black-and-white, and to draw some conclusions about what is going on.

One of my first stories as a young journalist was about a man wrongly convicted of murder. Even though numerous irregularities came to light during his trial, the jury still found him guilty.

Juries operate by consensus – every member must agree with the verdict. But juries can, and do, make mistakes In that trial forensic science was used improperly to secure a conviction. I learned then that science can be abused by people who have an agenda. Sometimes those people are police officers and prosecutors. Sometimes they are environmental activists and UN bureaucrats.

I helped keep the spotlight on that story until a man who had been imprisoned for a murder he did not commit was released, exonerated, and financially compensated.

In other words, I've held minority views before – and I know the world is capable of coming to its senses.

ACKNOWLEDGMENTS

For more than two years, I have been supported in large and small ways by people who helped make this book a reality.

My husband, Alan (*aka* my personal chef extraordinaire), has never faltered in his belief that this project was a worthy one despite the strain it has placed on our household finances. As James Delingpole has observed, writing that departs from the we're-all-going-to-die climate change narrative is:

> a journalist's nightmare. It's a journalist's bank manager's nightmare. Above all – just ask my wife – it's a journalist's spouse's nightmare. [see Chapter 4 of his book, *Watermelons*]

New ideas have a difficult time finding an audience. They take a while to gain traction. Because they are the opposite of what's fashionable, they are frequently dismissed out-of-hand.

Writing this book wasn't a smart economic move on my part, but I have been privileged to be married for more than two decades to a man of vision and integrity, who also happens to be my biggest fan.

~

Much of this book was written at the home of dear friends, Suzy and Darrel Miller, while they were away on their myriad adventures. They are extraordinary people who foster the arts as naturally as they breathe. Their abode is awash in colour and texture, and alive with creative energy Paintings, sculptures, photography, and music abound.

I shared many weeks with dear ol' Billy, their sweetheart of an 18-year-old dog, before he left us for that daisy-filled meadow in the sky. And I learned a thing or two about the demon that lurks behind the eyes of their dark-furred feline.

Elsewhere I've described how this book began as one project, became something different, and then evolved again. (The climate change story is so broad, so multi-faceted, and spans such a length of time that maintaining a single focus is difficult.) I've wrestled mightily with this manuscript. Without Suzy and Darrel's generosity – which included large bottles of red wine - these battles might not have been won.

~

While I live in the eastern part of Canada, blogger Hilary Ostrov resides on the west coast. We are separated by three time zones, but via the Internet and cheap long-distance telephone rates, have become fast friends. She has been a good-humored voice on the other end of the phone assuring me that I'm not losing my mind. Yes, moral indignation is appropriate under the circumstances. No, the explanations we're being given don't make sense.

Hilary single-handedly shook loose 678 pages worth of material on which this book relies. During its 2010 investigation of the IPCC, the InterAcademy Council committee posted an online questionnaire. We were told the responses would be made public, but months after the report was released that still hadn't occurred. Hilary tirelessly pursued the matter until some (but not all) of these responses were divulged.

From a journalist's perspective, they are solid gold – being the equivalent of interviews with dozens of people about their IPCC experiences. Until I read that material the IPCC was still a remote and confusing organization. By the time I'd finished, many more pieces of the puzzle had snapped into place.

In addition to being a grammar guru, a software wiz, and a fine editor, Hilary also participated in the development of a powerful research tool for those studying the IPCC. Thanks to her partnership with Australian programmer Peter Bobroff, there is now an annotated version of the 2007 report that highlights issues of concern. Visit it at: http://AccessIPCC.com/

~

In the old days, one drew-up a book outline, wrote some sample chapters, found a publisher to give you a contract and a cheque (*aka* an advance), and then withdrew to a quiet spot somewhere to finish the job.

But the chance of finding a publisher interested in an exposé of a UN body most people have never heard of isn't high. That this book also questions climate change dogma clinched the matter. In the foreword to his 2008 *An Appeal to Reason: A Cool Look at Global Warming*, Nigel Lawson writes that although his previous three books "had no difficulty whatever" finding a UK publisher, that particular manuscript "was rejected by every British publisher to whom it was submitted – and there were a considerable number of them."

During the time I was researching and writing this book, therefore, I was also blogging on a regular basis at NoFrakkingConsensus.com. This seemed to be a sensible way to build an audience for a book I intended to publish directly via Amazon.com - and that I would bear sole responsibility for marketing.

What I didn't anticipate was that my audience would become such a tremendous source of assistance and encouragement. More than 40 people from 12 countries volunteered their time to the Citizen Audit – a project I could not have completed on my own. I therefore owe a debt of gratitude to Anonymous, Anonymous2, Gordon Andelin, Bob Ashworth, Alexandra Belaire, Hazel Brown, David Bruce, Darko Butina, C3 Editor, Jennifer M. Cohen, Herve Deveaux, P. Gosselin, Gurgeh, Dann Gustavson, J. Harris, Harry, Robert Herron, Tim Hulsey, Mike Jowsey, Les Johnson, Jane Kerr,

Mark L., David Lee, Michael E. McKee, Riku Mellin, Sarie Moolman, John Moore, Richard C. Myer, Hilary Ostrov, Larry Pope, Dan Rempel, Tom Reeher, D. Robinson, Jchn Salmi, Sam at ClimateQuotes.com, Andy Scrase, Michael A. Saunders, southfarthing, Oguzhan Tandogac, TTY, Redmond Weissenberger and Danny Weston.

During December 2010 I ran an appeal on my blog in which I invited people to buy me a holiday cocktail via a small financial donation. Scores of people from America, Australia, Canada, Germany, Hong Kong, The Netherlands, Singapore, Sweden, Switzerland, and the United Kingdom generously responded. The messages that accompanied these donations continue to feed my soul. Again and again these people thanked me for my research efforts. They said I was performing a valuable public service - and helping to restore their faith in journalists. Because I didn't inquire at the time whether it would be OK to publicize their names, I am not doing so here. But I remain profoundly grateful to each of them and hope this book lives up to their expectations.

(In this regard it's worth mentioning that the focus and content of this book is highly strategic. This is not a catalog of every bad thing the IPCC has ever done. Rather, it is an argument. I have chosen my examples with care, selecting ones I thought might be easily digested by the average person who knows little about the climate debate.

In my mind's eye I am addressing an audience of ordinary citizens and the questions under discussion are: *What is the IPCC?* and *Can it be trusted?* I've marshaled my evidence and ordered my argument in the way that seemed to me to have the greatest chance of persuading a reasonable person with an open mind that this organization wields an inappropriate level of influence over our lives – and that it has a credibility score of zero.)

~

Several people paid me the enormous compliment of reading early drafts of this book. Their insight and enthusiasm helped sharpen and strengthen my arguments and helped spot typos, grammatical errors, factual errors, broken hyper-links, and other problems. The errors that remain are my responsibility entirely.

Among these wonderful people were Ron Albertson, Mark Bourrie, Albert Butterfield, Louise Butterfield, Bob Carter, Licia Carvello, Jamie Craig, Elaine Dean, Jan Dean, James Delingpole, Tom Fuller, Tim Hulsey, Nic Lewis, John McLean, Ross McKitrick, Elizabeth Nickson, Hilary Ostrov, Ben Pile, Sam, Glen Spooner, Sayward Spooner, Matt Ridley, Oggi Tandogac, Richard Tol, Redmond Weissenberger, and Toby Yull.

~

At a critical juncture in this book's development I was provided with a quiet working space by Fran and Tom Johnson, some of the dearest people in my life. Terry and Dave have been kind in numerous ways, including mowing my lawn and letting me use their swimming pool. Chris Stewart is my idea of an open-minded educator, and Tony & Mary have been warm and lovely.

~

Anya Shvetsova designed the two versions of this book's cover (one for the e-book and another for the paperback edition). In a competition hosted by 99designs.com her submission was elegant, evocative, and original.

~

I owe special thanks to Mike LaSalle, the publisher of MensNewsDaily.com, who extends the reach of my NoFrakkingConsensus.com blog by hosting my content there.

Moreover, my blog has been linked to by other bloggers and websites - to each of whom I hereby send a huge bouquet of thanks. Among them are American Thinker, Achgut.com, Australian Climate Madness, Autonomous Mind, Biased BBC, Bishop Hill, Blazing Cat Fur, Bourque Newswatch, C3Headlines.com, Cartoons by Josh, Celestial Junk, Climate Audit, Climate Change Dispatch, Climate Common Sense,

Climate Debate Daily, Climate Depot, Climate Etc., Climate Lessons, Climate Realists, Climate-Resistance.org, The Cimate Scam, Climate Science, Climate Skeptic Shop, The Common Room, Coyote Blog, The Daily Bayonet, A Few Figs, Five Feet of Fury, The Galileo Movement, The Global Warming Policy Foundation, Greenie Watch, Haunting the Library, The Hockey Schtick, IceCap, I Love Carbon Dioxide.com, James Delingpole, Jennifer Marohasy, Jerry Pournelle, JoNova, Junk Science Sidebar, Mark Lynas, National Newswatch, New Zealand Climate Science Ccalition, NoTricksZone, Prison Planet, Rational Optimist, Real Climategate, Richard Tol, ScottishSceptic, Shub Niggurath Climate, Small Dead Animals, Tom Nelson, The View from Here, WattsUpWithThat? and William M. Briggs. My apologies to the many others I've missed.

Blog readers have also directed a continuous stream of helpful, encouraging, and informative e-mails my way. Although I have not always managed to respond to these e-mails in a timely fashion, I appreciate them immensely.

In short, it takes a village to write a book - and my village is a vibrant one.

THE CITIZEN AUDIT

Introduction

The Citizen Audit was a fact-checking exercise conducted over five weeks in March and April 2010. My call for volunteers was answered by more than 40 private citizens from 12 countries.

Rajendra Pachauri, the chairman of the IPCC, has repeatedly claimed that the Climate Bible relies solely, entirely, and exclusively on peer-reviewed source material. Moreover, he has declared that non-peer-reviewed research is unworthy of the IPCC's attention and deserves to be tossed "into the dustbin."

Prior to our audit, no news agency, science body, government department, or think tank had gone to the trouble of checking whether Pachauri's public statements were actually supported by the facts.

When I discovered that two chapters of the 2007 Climate Bible relied on a significant number of sources that were not peer-reviewed scholarly papers, the question then became: To what degree were these two chapters representative of all 44 chapters?

I devised a methodology - a set of guidelines - by which to conduct a wider investigation. The references at the end of each chapter were examined by three citizen auditors working independently of each other. Only after the final results were released did they learn who else had audited that chapter. These volunteers sorted references into two categories - scholarly journal articles and everything else - and then reported the totals. When their findings differed slightly, we used the number most favorable to the IPCC. This wasn't about nitpicking, it was about the big picture.

At the time the 2007 report was written, the IPCC had a policy requiring non-peer-reviewed source material to be clearly designated as such when included in its reference lists. Had that policy been followed our audit would not have been necessary.

It is perhaps worth mentioning that our methodology was not the only one that could have been used. If we had had access to training seminars, funding, or oodles of time a more sophisticated approach might have been developed.

Summary of Findings

UN's Climate Bible Gets 21 'F's on Report Card

- all 18,531 references cited in the 2007 IPCC report were examined
- 5,587 are not peer-reviewed
- IPCC chairman's claim that the report relies solely on peer-reviewed sources is not supported
- each chapter was audited three times; the result most favorable to the IPCC was used
- 21 out of 44 chapters contain so few peer-reviewed references, they get an F (59% and below)
- 43 citizen auditors in 12 countries participated in this project

Main Findings

Grade	Chapters (out of 44)	% of Chapters receiving this grade
A (90 - 100%)	8	18%
B (80 - 89%)	5	11%
C (70 - 79%)	6	14%
D (60 - 69%)	4	9%
F (59% and below)	21	48%

Detailed Findings

2007 IPCC report (AR4)	% of references not peer-reviewed	number not peer-reviewed	total references
report overall	30	5,587	18,531
Working Group 1	7	431	6,226
Working Group 2	34	2,849	8,272
Working Group 3	57	2,307	4,033

Additional details are available at: **NOconsensus.org/ipcc-audit/IPCC-report-card.php** and **NOconsensus.org/ipcc-audit/findings-detailed.php**

Each of the three audits conducted for each of the 44 chapters is linked to in the online tables - click **a**, **b**, and **c** beneath the chapter names appearing here: **NOconsensus.org/ipcc-audit/findings-detailed.php**

The Citizen Audit report was released online on April 14, 2010.

A WORD ABOUT MY EVIDENCE

When the subject under discussion is controversial and the stakes are high, we should all be wary of taking anyone's word for it.

Although it is time-consuming, I strive to back-up every factual statement with a direct link to its source so that readers may readily verify matters for themselves. This standard of proof is much higher than that provided by a typical newspaper, news magazine, or television broadcast. It is also higher than that found in many books.

A good example is Thomas Friedman's 2008 *Hot, Flat and Crowded: Why We Need a Green Revolution - and How it Can Renew America*. Page 125 of that bestseller appears to be the origin of the oft-repeated John Holdren 'immense edifice' quote from which Chapter 9 of my book takes its title. But the context in which Holdren made these comments is far from clear. Was it in a public speech? A private conversation? In what year did he utter these words? Friedman tells us none of these.

In my view it is troubling that so many people were prepared to take Friedman's word for thousands of other assertions as well. In a review for Slate.com Gregg Easterbrook points out that it is difficult to verify any claim that appears in *Hot, Flat, and Crowded*:

Friedman embraces worst-case scenarios for climate change, warning not just of global warming but "global weirding." Yet his factual assertions are impossible to weigh, since *Hot, Flat, and Crowded* contains no footnotes or source notes...Friedman devotes several pages to asserting that the strength of Hurricane Katrina was caused by greenhouse gases, a claim that is first sourced to "many climatologists," none of whom he pauses to name; later in the book, his authority is a climate analyst for the Weather Channel. That global warming causes strong hurricanes, however, is far from a settled scientific view. [Friedman's 2008 book makes no mention of hurricane expert Chris Landsea's 2004 withdrawal from the IPCC.]

In sharp contrast, the e-book version of the title you are now reading (which currently sells for $4.99 on Amazon. com) links you to the speeches, advocacy publications, news articles, scientific papers, and IPCC documents discussed. Unlike Friedman, I back-up my assertions. Moreover, the vast majority of my sources are freely available on the Internet. There is no need for readers to travel to a well-resourced reference library to verify most of my claims.

This approach, I might observe, is eminently more user-friendly than the one adopted by the IPCC itself. At the time the 2007 Climate Bible was produced there was no reason why links to much of the IPCC's source material could not have been embedded into the online version of that report. But that raises another problem. Much of the scientific literature cited by the IPCC is behind paywalls. Scientific journals - including *Science*, which is published by the non-profit American Association for the Advancement of Science - charge members of the public $15 to $35 to view a single scholarly paper.

This means the average person has no meaningful access to the vast majority of the material on which the IPCC builds its case. Once again, we're expected to take the IPCC's word for it that the source material actually says what IPCC authors say it does. Once again we're left wondering why, if science academies around the world sincerely believe the planet is in peril, they haven't used their influence to ensure that everyone has access to all of the scholarly material on which the IPCC bases its findings.

My more accessible approach has a downside, however. Content on the Internet is often transient. Academic bios get moved to different web addresses. Newspapers take down older articles. Text on websites is updated with newer text.

Citing sources on the Internet is therefore a tricky business. In this book I make use of a valuable public service provided by WebCitation.org. This service makes a (time-stamped) copy of a webpage and then stores that copy so it can be referenced even if the original page disappears.

That this is an important and necessary service is demonstrated by the fact that the statement originally published at OpenLetterFromScientists.com has now vanished (see Chapter 13 and Chapter 14 of this book). Clicking on that web address currently brings one to an entirely unrelated page of German-language text. A record still survives, however, because I used WebCitation to make a copy of the original webpage.

WebCitation appears to be associated with the International Internet Preservation Consortium, which is led by senior librarians from around the world. Like other online services, however, it occasionally suffers from software and hardware glitches - and can also be sluggish. This means that sometimes documents I've linked to are temporarily unavailable.

If you experience outages or delays while attempting to access a web address that looks something like this **http://www.webcitation.org/XXXXX** please be patient and try again later.

The links in this book were double-checked by a third party. For a brief period, the person doing the verification reported that WebCitation was serving up the wrong documents. Later, however, matters righted themselves and everything behaved the way it is supposed to.

FOOTNOTES

<u>Print edition note</u>

Both the Kindle and PDF edition of this book (which retail for $4.99) contain more than 1,400 embedded hyperlinks that take readers directly to my source material. The footnotes below are an edited version of the ones included in the digital editions.

Purchase the PDF at: **TinyUrl.com/ipcc-expose**

The Kindle edition of *The Delinquent Teenager* is available at **Amazon.com** as well as at Amazon stores in the UK, Germany, and France.

at an event celebrating the IPCC's 20th anniversary General Ban Ki-moon said the occasion "to acknowledge the *proud parents* of this institution, the UN Environment Programme and the World Meteorological Organization, for the vision and foresight they had to establish the IPCC in 1988 by a General Assembly resolution." (italics added)

2-1
See the list of quotes about the IPCC at NOconsensus.org/ IPCC-quotes.php. Many are from the media, others are from IPCC participants, politicians, and activist groups.

- phenomenally successful (Stephen Schneider, *Science as a Contact Sport*, 2009, p. 125)
- a remarkable history of accomplishments (UN Secretary General Ban Ki-moon speech, 31 August 2008, p. 1 and p. 3)
- there is not a parallel on this planet, in any field of endeavour (Rajendra Pachauri, Rediff.com, 5 June 2007)
- its place in the history books is clear (UNEP head Achim Steiner speech, 31 August 2008, p. 3
- if the IPCC says something, you had better believe it (Tim Flannery, *The Weather Makers*, 2005, p. 246)

2-2
See the list of quotes about the IPCC at NOconsensus.org/ IPCC-quotes.php.

- the IPCC...has shown us the way (Bryan Walsh, *Time*, 9 December 2007)
- It is chapter and verse, it is Holy Writ (Mike McCarthy, Irish *Independent*, 19 November 2007)
- most scientists have been awed by the IPCC's deliberate work (Elisabeth Rosenthal and James Kanter, *New York Times*, 18 November 2007)

- The greatest feat of global scientific cooperation ever seen...utterly unique and authoritative (Damian Carrington, UK *Guardian*, 28 July 2011)

2-3

The speech by the Chairman of the Norwegian Nobel Committee was delivered in Oslo in December 2007. Read it here: Webcitation.org/**626BtZzf9**

2-4

Regarding Canada being 97% covered by ice see here: WebCitation.org/**626CRiee9**

3-1

See also the list of IPCC-related quotes at: NOconsensus.org/IPCC-quotes.php

- can't think of a better set of qualified people (interview with Rediff.com, June 2007)
- thousands of the best scientists (speech in Poznan, Poland; 1 December 2008, p. 1)
- the best scientific expertise from around the world (interview with *The Progressive*, May 2009)
- almost four thousand of the world's best specialists (speech, 22 September 2009, p. 1)

3-2

The full text of the 1995 IPCC health chapter is here: Tinyurl.com/**IPCC-health-1995** At the bottom of page 571 (page 11 of the PDF), it reads: "Although anopheline mosquito species that transmit malaria do not usually survive where the mean winter temperature drops below 16-18°C, some higher-latitude species are able to hibernate in sheltered sites."

Re: malaria in a historical context, see:
- WebCitation.org/ **61BPoHDZF**
- TinyUrl.com/**malaria-Shakespeare**
- WebCitation.org/**6242hqyS7**

4-1

Large IPCC reports are known as assessments. There have been four so far - dated 1990, 1995, 2001, and 2007. In this book they are called the Climate Bible. The IPCC has also produced a number of smaller reports on specific topics. Klein has participated in, and counts both, in his total.

5-1

The background to the establishment of the 2010 Inter-Academy Council (IAC) committee is discussed in Chapter 33. The short version is that it was a response on the part of the UN and the IPCC to the Himalayan glacier scandal - one of the few occasions in which some parts of the mainstream media covered the IPCC in a properly skeptical fashion.

Another view of the 2010 IAC investigation of the IPCC is presented in Ross McKitrick's *Reforming the IPCC: Why and How* published by the Global Warming Policy Foundation. (As this book went to press McKitrick's report was scheduled for release in late 2011; the quote below is from a pre-publication copy and should be double-checked against the final version.) McKitrick observes:

> At the time of its selection, the IAC did not have any track record in evaluation of agency procedures, nor was it credibly independent of the IPCC. Prior to the 2010 IPCC Review its most recent report was a 2007 study promoting alternative energy, coauthored by a 15-member committee that included IPCC Chair Rajendra Pachauri, and IPCC Lead Authors Nebosja Nakicenovic and Ged Davis.

> The IAC Report did make some useful recommendations ...[but] should not, however, be considered as the last word on the subject of reforming the IPCC; in many respects it should only be seen as the first word.

5-2

The 678-page PDF containing the questionnaire answers is available at:
http://reviewipcc.interacademycouncil.net/Comments.pdf
Oddly, there is a discrepancy between the number of submissions publicly released and the number of people we were told provided input to the 2010 committee. See here: TinyUrl.com/**6bu3qle**

6-1

In an October 2002 document, Meinshausen is presented as a Greenpeace spokesperson and his contact info includes a Greenpeace e-mail address. In a June 2003 document, his affiliation is listed as Greenpeace International. In a December 2003 document, he is one of three Greenpeace International contact people listed at the bottom. See:

- WebCitation.org/**5x42Qb8RJ**
- WebCitation.org/**5x46RrRyK**
- TinyUrl.com/**3koev7c**

6-2

See the end of my blog post at: TinyUrl.com/**3gv42vx** for the nine Climate Bible chapters that list papers by Hoegh-Guldberg among their references.

6-3

A press release says Moss was appointed a WWF vice-president in November 2007. According to a bio: "During a business leave of absence from 2006-2009, he served as Vice President/Managing Director for Climate Change at WWF and Senior Director for Energy and Climate at the U.N. Foundation." As of August 2011, the WWF website still listed Moss as a WWF 'Senior Fellow, Climate Change.'

In June 2009 Moss participated in a meeting in which he represented both the WWF and the IPCC's Task Group on Data and Scenarios for Impact and Climate Analysis. In June 2010, the IPCC appointed him a Review Editor for the upcoming edition of the Climate Bible. See:

- WebCitation.org/**618C4UDUu**
- WebCitation.org/**5yD9p2GVH**
- WebCitation.org/**618CUDdLt**
- WebCitation.org/**619nDmlL9**
- NOconsensus.org/AR5_authors.pdf

Review editors are not discussed elsewhere in this book. They come into the picture when external expert reviewers are asked to provide feedback on what IPCC authors have written (see Chapter 11, Chapter 14, and Chapter 33). In theory, review editors are supposed to ensure that reviewers' comments are accorded due consideration and that a wide spectrum of scientific thought is reflected in the text of their chapter. This is one of the mechanisms by which the IPCC says it avoids bias.

But as the 2010 InterAcademy Council committee reported, review editors can be overruled by a chapter's authors and therefore have no real power.

In other words, supposed IPCC checks-and-balances are toothless and illusory - and have been that way for two decades.

6-4

A 1976 book titled *RIO: Reshaping the International Order* was prepared for the Club of Rome. On page 133 (Chapter 7, section 5) this book speaks approvingly of the emergence of full-blown activist scientists by the mid-1970s:

> In the past, [scientists] have often been reluctant to engage in political debate or to share their knowledge and fears with the general public. Given social dilemmas, they have often preferred to adopt neutral rather than value positions, to tacitly advise rather than openly advocate. This generalization no longer holds true. **In many branches of science there are radical movements**. **Increasingly**, both in the rich and poor worlds, **scientists are involved in active advocacy** which they see as an intellectual and ethical duty. [bold added]

See a photo of that page at: TinyUrl.com/**radical-scientists**

6-5

Oppenheimer served in six distinct capacities connected to the 2007 Climate Bible. He was a contributing author for Chapter 2 and a lead author for Chapter 19 of the Working Group 2 report. He helped write Working Group 2's *Summary for Policymakers* as well as its *Technical Summary*. He is also listed as an expert reviewer for the Working Group 1 report and an expert reviewer of the summary of summaries known as the *Synthesis Report.*

7-1

Climate activists frequently talk about the fact that CO_2 could double - from 0.03% to 0.06% of the atmosphere. That sounds significant. But if your chance of catching a cold increases from one chance in a hundred to two chances in a hundred the risk remains small even though it has, indeed, doubled. The important question is whether the change is meaningful.

Smart, experienced, trustworthy scientists remain divided on the question of whether a doubling of CO_2 in the atmosphere is something about which we should get alarmed. Just because there is a dominant/fashionable position does not mean that those with less fashionable views are wrong. As Roy Spencer, a meteorologist with 40 years experience (who is also the recipient of NASA's Exceptional Scientific Achievement Medal) has written on this topic: an increase in a very small number "is still a very small number."

7-2

These days Zwiers and Hegerl are better known for their work with statistics. But Zwiers headed Canada's "flagship climate modelling research laboratory" between 1997 and 2006. During the 1990s, many of Hegerl's earliest published papers focussed on climate model simulations. See:

- WebCitation.org/**612NjJByg**
- WebCitation.org/**623s6e8hq**

8-1

A 27-page PDF at **NOconsensus.org/AR5_authors.pdf** lists the authors of the IPCC's upcoming report. It is a compilation of three separate lists (one for each of three IPCC working groups) that were released by the IPCC in June 2010.

On page eight of the PDF, the IPCC begins supplying university and other affiliations. By page 20, it has reverted back to names and nations only. In other words, only Working Group 2 volunteered a small amount of additional info when it made its list of names public.

As this book went to press Hilary Ostrov drew my attention to an updated list. I had no opportunity to examine it, but it can be seen here: **WebCitation.org/623sTasdY**

9-1

From Garth Paltridge's book, *The Climate Caper*. The quote about peer reviewers appears in Chapter 6, in the section titled *Uncertainty and the High Moral Ground*.

9-2

The discussion about published papers being merely advertising appears on page 5 here: WebCitation.org/**5r4Q8z4Ne**

9-3

The 678 pages of collected questionnaire answers are here: **http://reviewipcc.interacademycouncil.net/comments.html**

On page 99 someone says: "the needs of the IPCC for data quality assurance substantially exceed the needs for journal publications."

See also page 362 where someone adds: "we generally do not have peer review processes for major data holdings – just because there is a quality publication from a dataset does not mean all the underlying data are good."

10-1

Here are three Seth Borenstein articles from early 2007:

- WebCitation.org/**60reCv7VX**
- WebCitation.org/**5yPkwDl5H**
- Webcitation.org/**5yQ18Frjn**

The first says the about-to-be-released Working Group 1 report "will draw on already published peer-review science.' The second says the IPCC "used only peer-reviewed published science." According to the third: "**More than** 2,500 scientists worldwide contributed to the report, **relying on peer-reviewed studies** to make their findings and **subjecting them several times to outside review**." [all bolding inserted by me]

As becomes clear in the next chapter, only two out of three references in the 2007 Climate Bible are actually to peer-reviewed studies.

The Working Group 1 report scored highest in this regard, but 431 of the sources on which it relied were not published in peer-reviewed journals. Moreover, 34% of the references in Working Group 2 and 57% in Working Group 3 were to non-peer-reviewed material.

In total, non-peer-reviewed sources appeared in the IPCC's references nearly 5,600 times. (See these numbers in easy-to-digest tables in the Citizen Audit section of this book, beginning on page 184.)

The IPCC says there were 450 lead authors plus 800 contributing authors involved. (See the graphic here: WebCitation.org/**60rgQGh7t**) That makes 1,250 contributors. Borenstein reported *more than* 2,500.

The IPCC claims there were an *additional* 2,500 *expert reviewers*. As I explain elsewhere in this book, the IPCC is exaggerating the number of expert reviewers since it isn't unusual for IPCC authors to also serve as expert reviewers - which means they get counted at least twice.

Chapter 14 of this book demonstrates that the IPCC's review process is far from airtight and that nothing prevents IPCC authors from rejecting reviewer comments out-of-hand. Chapter 33 explains why the review process is not independent. Borenstein makes no mention of these issues.

The IPCC solicited feedback from external reviewers on two occasions; Borenstein says there were *several* rounds of review.

The reviewers read drafts of the IPCC report. Borenstein, however, implies that reviewers examined the thousands of peer-reviewed *studies* on which the report relies. While it's true all of those studies were theoretically available to reviewers, there's no way to know how many were actually scrutinized. Even when every book in the library can be borrowed, not all of them are taken off the shelf.

In 2008 the Society of Environmental Journalists awarded Borenstein first prize in the *Outstanding Beat Reporting* category for his 2007 coverage of the IPCC.

11-1
For more info, see the Citizen Audit section of this book, beginning on page 184.

Pachauri said the IPCC cited "approximately 18,000 peer-reviewed publications." I suspect what he meant is that, when one counts all the entries in the reference lists at the end of all the IPCC chapters one arrives at the number 18,531.

It may or may not be true that there are 18,000 *different* publications. As we see in Chapter 14, a single information source - the Stern Review - was cited by the IPCC in 12 different chapters. This means it was listed among the references at the end of each and counted 12 times. A far larger problem is that the IPCC cites its own reports *ad nauseam*. Most IPCC chapters include multiple references to a body of IPCC-generated literature that is counted again and again.

During the Citizen Audit it also became apparent that an identical piece of research is often described differently in these reference lists. Here, for example, is how an IPCC-produced document is cited by the IPCC in the reference lists of Chapter 1 of Working Group 1, Chapter 2 of WG1, Chapter 3 of WG1, Chapter 10 of WG1, and Chapter 5 of WG3 respectively:

- IPCC, 1999: *Special Report on Aviation and the Global Atmosphere* [Penner, J.E., et al. (eds.)]. Cambridge University Press, Cambridge, United Kingdom and New York, NY, USA, 373 pp.
- IPCC, 1999: *Aviation and the Global Atmosphere: A Special Report of IPCC Working Groups I and III* [Penner, J.E., et al. (eds.)]. Cambridge University

Press, Cambridge, United Kingdom and New York, NY, USA, 373 pp.

- IPCC, 1999: *Aviation and the Global Atmosphere* [Penner, J. E., et al. (eds.)]. Cambridge University Press, Cambridge, United Kingdom and New York, NY, USA, 384pp.
- Penner, J.E., et al. (eds.), 1999: *Aviation and the Global Atmosphere*. Cambridge University Press, Cambridge, United Kingdom and New York, NY, USA, 373 pp.
- IPCC, 1999: *Aviation and the Global Atmosphere* [Penner, J.E., D.H. Lister, D.J. Griggs, D.J. Dokken and M. McFarland (eds)]. Special report of the Intergovernmental Panel on Climate Change (IPCC) Working Groups I and III, Cambridge University Press, Cambridge.

No two citations are the same. It remains uncertain, therefore, how many distinct publications were actually referenced by the 2007 Climate Bible.

Regarding Pachauri's claim that non-peer-reviewed literature was cited by the IPCC when peer-reviewed was unavailable, this is an appropriate time to remind ourselves that the spark that ignited the Citizen Audit was a blog post by Richard Tol which complained that IPCC authors had ignored the findings of peer-reviewed literature - choosing instead to cite non-peer-reviewed material that came to the opposite conclusion.

In Chapter 28 of the book you are currently reading Roger Pielke Jr. raises the same concern He says "Plenty of peer-reviewed work" comes to unambiguous conclusions about natural disaster damages - yet the IPCC highlighted a single *non-peer-reviewed* paper to support a contrary position.

12-1

A 2009 open letter organized by the World Wildlife Fund and signed by Canadian scientists may be seen here: **http://wwf.ca/conservation/global_warming/scientists_voice.cfm** On the right-hand side of that page, the WWF says the letter appeared in two Canadian newspapers.

A 2008 letter from Canadian scientists organized by the activist group Climate Action Network Canada was published on the website of the Canadian Broadcasting Corporation (CBC). Another copy, including the names of those who signed, is here: WebCitation.org/**61ud4jUai**

A 2006 open letter from Canadian scientists, agreeing with the 2001 IPCC report, appears here: WebCitation.org/ **60We7Asvo**

A 2009 letter from UK scientists affirming the IPCC's 2007 findings may be examined at: WebCitation.org/ **60WdkdTyp**. In that case, the letter appears to have been organized by a government body.

A 2010 open letter published in the journal *Science* may be seen here: WebCitation.org/**623tQF72D**

A 2010 letter of support for the IPCC was posted on a website with the now-defunct domain name OpenLetterFrom Scientists.com. A backup copy can be perused here: Web Citation.org/**5wcI1dRhn** Another copy of the letter, posted by a blogger, is here: http://**mind.ofdan.ca/?p=2901**

Still another open letter from scientists to the US Congress appeared in 2011. See it here: WebCitation.org/**60srkXlfo**

Finally, here are two other open letters. The first, dated March 2010 and organized by the activist Union of Concerned Scientists, is here: http://www.usclimatenetwork.org /resource-database/ucs-letter-to-congress-potect-the-caa

The second is dated June 2011 and is signed by Australian scientists: WebCitation.org/**61fbngUBv**

13-1
The final version of the InterAcademy Council report, dated October 2010, is available at:
http://reviewipcc.interacademycouncil.net/report.html
The "few instances of information flagged" quote appears on page 35 of the PDF, which is numbered as page 17 within the document.

13-2
The full InterAcademy Council report is available at: **http://reviewipcc.interacademycouncil.net/report.html**
The "strengthen and enforce" as well as the "appropriately

flagged" quotes appear in the shaded box on page 35 of the PDF, which is numbered as page 17 within the document.

13-3
The 678 pages of collected questionnaire answers are available as a PDF at :
http://reviewipcc.interacademycouncil.net/comments.ht ml. See pages 41 (italics), 115 (asterisks), and 396 (different colors).

13-4
The document containing this discussion is a 267-page PDF available here:
http://www.ipcc.ch/meetings/session33/inf01_p33_revie w_report_tg_comments_gov.pdf

13-5
A May 2010 press release says the IPCC has adopted new literature rules, yet makes no mention of the flagging-grey-literature issue. See it here: WebCitation.org/**61CUnZZnM**

As blogger Hilary Ostrov discovered, flagging was definitely abandoned. See TinyUrl.com/**lets-disappear-it**

The mainstream media failed to notice - much less report on - this blatant flouting of an InterAcademy Council committee recommendation. (The committee's full report is available at: **http://reviewipcc.interacademycouncil.net/ report.html** See the shaded box on page 35 of the PDF.)

Incidentally, the IPCC press release made a point of mentioning that the new literature rules regard blogs as "not acceptable sources of information for IPCC reports" - even though climate-related blogs such as Anthony Watts' WattsUpWithThat, Steve McIntyre's ClimateAudit, Judith Curry's Climate Etc., Lucia's The Blackboard and many others have made important contributions to the climate debate.

It wasn't blogs that led to the Himalayan glacier mistake discussed in Chapter 33 of this book, but a World Wildlife Fund report. The IPCC, however, hasn't learned its lesson. The same rules that go out of their way to disqualify blogs failed to forbid the use of publications produced by groups such as the WWF and Greenpeace.

16-1

Stephen Schneider was an American physicist. As early as 1976 he'd authored a book dramatically subtitled: *Climate and Global Survival*. The journal *Climatic Change* commenced publishing shortly afterward, in March 1977.

16-2

One of the 16 papers was accepted in May 2006 - well past Pachauri's "prior to January 2006" cutoff date, but still early enough that an expert reviewer who asked for it could have received a copy.

16-3

The IPCC released the names of the authors for its Fifth Assessment Report (AR5) in June 2010. See the 27-page PDF at **NOconsensus.org/AR5_authors.pdf.** On page 7 we read that Danish climate modeler Jens Hesselbjerg Christensen is now a coordinating lead author of Chapter 14.

17-1

Johnston's 82-page paper may be read online at TinyUrl. com/**advocacy-science**.

- "unbiased and objective..." appears on page 8 of the PDF (numbers printed on the page differ slightly)
- "such verification means..." p. 8
- "on virtually every major issue...systematically conceal..." p. 9
- "scientists at the very best universities..." p. 11
- "something is wrong with the models..." p. 22
- isn't even mentioned is my paraphrase of Johnston's "no mention is made" which appears on p. 22

17-2

Johnston's 82-page paper may be read online at TinyUrl. com/**advocacy-science**.

- "output of climate analysis..." appears on page 25 of the PDF
- "no mention whatsoever..." p. 27

18-1

Garth Paltridge's quote about the fallout from his media interview appears early in Chapter 4 of *The Climate Caper*. See also the section "Too Many Scientists" in Chapter 5.

20-1

Article 2 of the UNFCCC says the ultimate objective of that treaty is the "stabilization of greenhouse gas concentrations in the atmosphere at a level that would prevent dangerous [human-caused] interference with the climate system."

This 1992 document takes it as a given that it is within humanity's power to 'stabilize' various gases in the atmosphere. But this always changing, continually evolving planet was dancing to its own drummer billions of years before we put in an appearance. One wonders whether the people who drafted this treaty considered the possibility that human attempts to stabilize certain gases might, of its own accord, amount to dangerous interference with the climate system.

As of August 2011 there were 193 Kyoto Protocol signatories.

21-1

That green activists are permitted to witness these meetings but journalists are not is troubling. It means that one of the primary ways journalists glean the information necessary to write/broadcast their reports is by interviewing green activists.

Whether by accident or design, the current system virtually guarantees that whatever information the media has access to is heavily filtered - by the IPCC itself, and by people who have an activist agenda.

22-1

Australian Prime Minister Kevin Rudd's speech may be downloaded at **http://www.lowyinstitute.org/Publication.asp?pid=1167**

23-1

The Swedish advisory council's 169-page report is here: **http://www.sweden.gov.se/content/1/c6/09/46/09/f1b a24fc.pdf**. See page 50 of the PDF - numbered as p. 48 within the document.

24-1

On at least one edition of *A Blueprint for Survival*, the Sunday *Times* quote was given larger prominence than the title itself.

25-1

See WebCitation.org/**61ueFEbHI**. Pages 7-8 of this PDF are devoted to the thoughts of Pachauri, who is described as a plenary speaker and "Chairman, Nobel Prize-winning International Panel on Climate Change." The portions I've quoted appear on p. 8.

The PDF is Chapter 3 of a 2009 book produced by the Rockefeller Foundation following the Global Urban Summit held in Italy in July 2007.

26-1

For examples of activist groups promoting emissions reduction on a particular timetable see Greenpeace, StepItUp 2007, and Conservation Law Foundation material at:

- WebCitation.org/**604iBrfnV**
- Webcitation.org/**604hHfd1K**
- WebCitation.org/**5zlAU97IL**

27-1

Brian Hoskins was closely associated with Working Group 1 of the 2007 Climate Bible. He was a review editor for the Trenberth chapter, a lead author of the *Technical Summary*, and helped draft the *Summary for Policymakers*. He also served as an expert reviewer.

Hoskins is currently employed by the meteorology department at the University of Reading. He is a former president of the UK's Royal Meteorological Society (1998-2000) and a former president of the International Association of Meteorology and Atmospheric Sciences (1991-1995). In 2007 he was knighted.

While testifying before a House of Lords committee in 2004, Hoskins suggested that lobby groups may be pressuring individual scientists in an improper manner. In the highly politicized arena of climate change this is surely a serious concern. But there is little indication that he, or anyone else, has done much to make the public aware of this problem:

> I feel myself, having got close to the Intergovernmental Panel on Climate Change, that when you do mix scientists with policy then the special interest groups can put tremendous pressure on individual scientists. It is useful for the academies to provide a supporting role for colleagues who otherwise are seen as just an individual against a powerful lobby group.

Here, again, one wonders where the open letters are? What concrete steps has the scientific community taken to insulate its members from improper influence? Where is the public pushback against lobby groups by scientific bodies working hard to safeguard scientific integrity?

28-1

The IPCC discusses cyclones (hurricanes) three places in its *Synthesis Report* - the summary of summaries. Twice here: WebCitation.org/**61n4Pzcoq**, once here: WebCitation.org/ **61n4WcCUJ**

28-2

The consensus statement produced by the May 2006 workshop organized by Roger Pielke Jr. is available at: Web Citation.org/**603RjSF28**

Point #11 on page 5 of the PDF reads, in part: "it is still not possible to determine the portion of the increase in damages that might be attributed to climate change due to [greenhouse gas] emissions."

Point #13 on page 6 says, in part: "In the near future the quantitative link (attribution) of trends in storm and flood losses to climate changes related to [greenhouse gas] emissions is unlikely to be answered unequivocally."

28-3
See the mystery graph at: WebCitation.org/**60oJaSN3U**

29-1
Those in charge of IPCC chapters early in that organization's history were called convening lead authors rather than co-ordinating lead authors. That term is still used by individuals whose IPCC involvement dates back to that time.

29-2
See 11 instances here: TinyUrl.com/**planetary-overload-copy**

29-3
Re: malaria in a historical context, see:

- WebCitation.org/ **61BPoHDZF**
- TinyUrl.com/**malaria-Shakespeare,**
- WebCitation.org/**6242hqyS7,**
- WebCitation.org/**6242mPfWj**

29-4
The website of the *American Scientist* describes this publication as "an illustrated bimonthly magazine about science and technology." It is not an academic journal. Its articles are not peer-reviewed. The full citation for the article under discussion is as follows:

Levins, R., T. Awerbuch, U. Brinkman, I. Eckhardt, P.R. Epstein, N. Makhoul, C. Albuquerque de Possas, C. Puccia, A. Spielman, and M.E. Wilson, 1994: The emergence of new diseases. *American Scientist*, 82, 52-60.

30-1
Andrew Githeko completed his PhD in medical entomology in 1992 at the Liverpool School of Tropical Medicine. He became one of the Climate Bible's most senior authors in 1999.

30-2

There are strong parallels, as well, between how journalists covered Y2K and how they cover climate change. In January 1999 *Vanity Fair* magazine published an article titled *The Y2K Nightmare*. (See here: WebCitation.org/**60oODyUNQ**) The opening blurb read as follows:

> Will the millennium arrive in darkness and chaos as billions of lines of computer code containing two-digit year dates shut down hospitals, banks, police and fire departments, airlines, utilities, the Pentagon, and the White House? These nightmare scenarios are only too possible, Robert Sam Anson discovers as he traces the birth of the Y2K "bug," the folly, greed and denial that have muffled two decades of warnings from technology experts, and the ominous results of Y2K tests that lay bare the dimensions of a ticking global time bomb.

Notice the language. Nightmare scenarios. *Folly, greed* - and my personal favorite - *denial*. Warnings that are being ignored. *Ticking global time bomb.* All of these phrases are currently used by the media in its climate change coverage.

Please also note that the author of this piece, Robert Sam Anson, was no neophyte. He had been a journalist for more than three decades by the time he wrote that Y2K story.

Yet he still got it dreadfully wrong. For example, he told readers that the one sure thing was that machines would not know what to do after the clock struck midnight. He declared that some computers would *die* - as would *the blind faith the world has placed in them*. He suggested that Y2K-related lawsuits would total *$1 trillion in the United States alone*. But none of those things actually happened.

Journalists these days hype global warming by emphasizing how cruelly it will affect the developing world. In 1999 Anson advised readers that: "Y2K's impact on the delivery of food, seed, and fertilizer could result in between 10 million and 300 million deaths" in less fortunate nations. He quoted someone else who warned of "civil unrest" in such regions.

Anson surveyed a wide range of well-educated, influential people - scientists, economists, government officials, and IT specialists. They obliged by talking about an accidental nuclear war and "blood-in-the-streets." They declared that "our entire way of life is at risk" and predicted: "In the year 2000, Asia will be burnt toast."

According to US senator Chris Dodd there were three places no one should be on New Year's Eve 1999: "In an elevator; in an airplane, or in a hospital." (In 2007 Dodd spearheaded a climate change campaign targeting the Securities and Exchange Commission. By 2008 he was advocating a carbon tax as a way of averting "potentially devastating climate change.")

But the predictions of journalist Anson's vast array of eminent experts missed by a mile – or ten. The *looming disaster, potential catastrophe, misery*, economic *recession, potentially disastrous consequences*, and *impending doom* readers were warned about never came to pass.

One of those experts was Canada-based computer consultant named Peter de Jager. According to Anson, in the run-up to the turn of the millennium de Jager was delivering 85 speeches annually and "reportedly pulling in more than $1 million a year" by sounding the Y2K alarm. Anson quoted a 2003 column penned by de Jager that included these lines:

> Have you ever been in a car accident? Time seems to slow down...It's too late to avoid it - you're going to crash. All you can do now is watch it happen...We are heading toward the year 2000. We are heading toward a failure of our standard date format...Unfortunately, unlike the car crash, time will not slow down for us. If anything, **we're accelerating toward disaster**...We and our computers were supposed to make life easier. This was our promise. **What we have delivered is a catastrophe**. [bold added]

On page 27 of his 2009 book, *Flat Earth News*, Nick Davies reports that in early January 2000 de Jager admitted on his website that Italy, one of several countries that had devoted little attention (and few funds) to the Y2K issue, hadn't been reduced to a smoldering heap of ashes the way he'd imagined it would.

"My view of the problem is contradicted by a fact I cannot refute," de Jager acknowledged with some humility. "Italy has seen no significant effects...Countries that did nothing were faced with fewer problems than we expected."

So what did the media learn from the embarrassing Y2K episode? Judging by the way it proceeded to cover climate change, zilch. Nada. Nothing at all. Take a peek at this 2006 *Time* magazine story: WebCitation.org/**60oY1oXeQ** On a single page it shouts about Earth at the *tipping point*, declares that the planet is *ill, fragile, fighting a fever* and has *finally got a bellyful of us*.

The main image for that *Time* story, incidentally, was supplied by Greenpeace.

30-3

Medical doctor Jonathan Patz is described as a "UN IPCC Scientist" on a YouTube page. The video title reads: *An Interview with UN IPCC Scientist Dr. Jonathan Patz -1-1*.

A bio page for Patz at the University of Wisconsin-Madison lists (and links to) that video, thereby repeating the "UN IPCC Scientist" claim.

30-4

Paul Epstein has written about a wide range of topics:

- health consequences of war in Nicaragua (*The Lancet*, 29 June 1985)
- health service targets in Nicaragua (*The Lancet*, 12 Oct. 1985)
- mercury poisoning (*The Lancet*, 1 June 1991)
- Kurdish refugees (*Journal of the American Medical Association*, Aug. 1991)
- poverty and respiratory disease (*Seminars in Respiratory Infections*, Dec. 1991)
- pestilence and poverty (*American Journal of Preventative Medicine*, July-Aug. 1992)

- Soviet nuclear mishaps pre-Chernobyl (*The Lancet*, 6 Feb. 1993)

- cholera in west Africa (*The Lancet*, 3 Jan. 1998)
- disease-causing weeds in east Africa (*The Lancet*, 21 Feb. 1998)
- West Nile virus and climate (*Journal of Urban Health*, June 2001)
- swimming-related illnesses (*Environmental Health Perspectives*, July 2001)
- US drinking water challenges in the 21st century (*Environmental Health Perspectives*, Feb. 2002)
- global issues in medical education (*The Lancet*, 23 Feb. 2002)
- AIDS in Africa (*The Lancet*, 2 Nov. 2002)
- climate change and children's health (*Ambulatory Pediatrics*, Jan. 2003)

30-5
The full citation for the non-peer-reviewed, written-by-non-experts magazine article that claimed malaria has already spread as a result of global warming is as follows:

Levins, R., T. Awerbuch, U. Brinkman, I. Eckhardt, **P.R. Epstein**, N. Makhoul, C. Albuquerque de Possas, C. Puccia, A. Spielman, and M.E. Wilson, 1994: The emergence of new diseases. *American Scientist*, 82, 52-60.

The health chapter of the 1995 edition of the Climate Bible cited this article. Paul Epstein was a lead author of said chapter.

30-6
For the 1995 Climate Bible, Woodward was a contributing author. He then served as a review editor for the 2001 edition, before becoming a lead author for the 2007 edition.

While there is currently a second coordinating lead author - American microbiologist Rita Colwell - she appears to be a

212

- Rodel **Lasco** - a coordinating lead author who also helped write two summary documents for the 2007 report and is now a lead author
- Rik **Leemans** - a 2007 lead author who is now serving as a review editor
- Michael **MacCracken** - served as a 2007 contributing author, review editor and as an expert reviewer in three different capacities for the 2007 report - which makes five hats in total
- Dena P. **MacMynowski** - a 2007 contributing author for two chapters and expert reviewer
- José **Marengo** - a 2007 lead author who is currently a review editor
- Eric **Martin** - a 2007 lead author and expert reviewer who is serving once again as a lead author
- Mahmoud **Medany** - a 2007 coordinating lead author and lead author
- Claudio Guillermo **Menéndez** - who served as a lead author for the 2007 report
- Annette **Menzel** - a 2007 lead author
- Guy **Midgley** - a 2007 coordinating lead author who helped write two summary documents and is once again serving as a coordinating lead author
- Charles Kenneth **Minns** - a 2007 contributing author
- Monirul Qader **Mirza** - a 2007 coordinating lead author who wore four other hats for the 2007 report and is now serving as a lead author
- Alison **Misselhorn** - a 2007 contributing author
- Ana Rosa **Moreno** - a 2007 lead author, now review editor
- Mark **New** - a lead author for the 2007 report
- Shuzo **Nishioka** - a 2007 review editor

- Carlos **Nobre** - a 2007 lead author and currently a coordinating lead author
- Patrick **Nunn** - currently a lead author
- Leonard **Nurse** - a coordinating lead author who wore five other hats for the 2007 report and is once again a coordinating lead author
- Mark **Nuttal** - a 2007 lead author and expert reviewer
- Anthony **Nyong** - a coordinating lead author who wore four other hats for the 2007 report
- Govind Ballabh **Pant** - a 2007 review editor
- Barrie **Pittock** - a 2007 lead author & expert reviewer
- Batimaa **Punsalmaa** - a lead author for two chapters of the 2007 report
- N.H. **Ravindranath** - a 2007 lead author and expert reviewer who is again serving as a lead author
- George **Rose** - a 2007 lead author
- Joyashree **Roy** - a coordinating lead author who wore four other hats for the 2007 report and is once again serving as a coordinating lead author
- Victor Magaña **Rueda** - a 2007 lead author and expert reviewer
- Stephen **Schneider** - a 2007 coordinating lead author who wore four other hats. Prior to his death in 2010 he was again appointed a coordinating lead author
- Mohamed **Senouci** - a 2007 review editor
- Anond **Snidvongs** - a 2007 expert reviewer who is now a lead author
- Daithi **Stone** - wore seven hats for the 2007 Climate Bible, including lead author and expert reviewer for the *Synthesis Report* - and is once again a lead author

- John **Sweeney** - a 2007 review editor, contributing author, & expert reviewer for Working Group 1 & 2
- Piotr **Tryjanowski** - a 2007 lead author
- John **Turner** - a 2007 expert reviewer
- Riccardo **Valentini** - currently a coordinating lead author
- Jef **Vandenberghe** - a 2007 lead author and expert reviewer
- Richard **Washington** - a 2007 contributing author
- Poh Poh **Wong** - a coordinating lead author who served in three additional capacities for the 2007 report and is once again a coordinating lead author
- Gary **Yohe** - a coordinating lead author who served in four other capacities for the 2007 report. He is once again a coordinating lead author
- Zong-Ci **Zhao** - a 2007 lead author currently serving as a review editor
- Gina **Ziervogel** - a 2007 contributing author and expert reviewer

The web address for the WWF panel is Tinyurl.com/ **WWF-SAP**. The names of those working on the upcoming edition of the Climate Bible may be seen here: **NOconsensus.org/AR5_authors.pdf**

32-1

Ross McKitrick, in his paper, *What is the 'Hockey Stick' Debate About?* explains:

The hockey stick graph...was central to the 2001 [IPCC report]. It appears as Figure 1b in the Working Group 1 Summary for Policymakers, Figure 5 in the Technical Summary, twice in Chapter 2 (Figures 2-20 and 2-21) of the main report, and Figures 2-3 and 9-1B in the Synthesis Report. Referring to this figure, the IPCC Summary for Policymakers (p. 3) claimed it is likely "that the 1990s has been the warmest decade and 1998 the warmest year of the millennium" for the Northern Hemisphere.

(See WebCitation.org/**623pAU652** for McKitrick's paper.)
Some examples of the hockey stick in official documents:

- a Swedish Environmental Protection Agency publication intended to communicate the IPCC's 2001 findings to a general audience (see p. 9 of the PDF here: TinyUrl.com/**Swedish-EPA**)
- a New Zealand Ministry of the Environment flyer here: WebCitation.org/**609dSWOgh**
- a 2003 US government *Strategic Plan for the Climate Change Science Program* here: WebCitation.org /**609ecU40d**
- an Australian government publication (p. 4 of the PDF here: WebCitation.org/609fAGj3M
- French and Canadian government websites here: WebCitation.org/**60FjoH1IM** and here: WebCitation.org/**6245S3yY3**
- the website of the European Environment Agency: Webcitation.org/**60FkDHyiv**

32-2
Regarding Wikipedia and climate change, see *How Wikipedia's green doctor rewrote 5,428 climate articles*. It reports that a single individual - U.K. scientist and Green Party activist William Connolley - created or re-wrote 5,428 Wikipedia entries, deleted 500 more, and was responsible for having 2,000 other Wikipedia contributors banned. See: WebCitation.org /**6245mkwJ1**.
See also: WebCitation.org/**6245qyHW7** and **http:// energy.probeinternational.org/search/node/wikipedia**

32-3

The bottom graph on page 8 at: WebCitation.org/
623pAU652 presents the traditional perspective on temperature, as per the IPCC's 1990 report.

32-4

The audio recording of Don Easterbrook's remarks appears to
have been removed from the Heartland.org website between
the time the digital edition of this book was fact-checked and
this print edition was being prepared. A similar, written
account appears here: TinyUrl.com/**Easterbrook**

32-5

See the bottom of page 2 at: WebCitation.org/**61zHysZHp**
for more info about the flyer sent to Canadian homes.

32-6

My account of Steve McIntyre and Ross McKitrick's work is
based on McKitrick's paper *What is the 'Hockey Stick' Debate
About?* See especially the second half of page 7 and the top of
page 8: WebCitation.org/**61zHysZHp**

32-7

Ross McKitrick, in his paper *What is the Hockey Stick' Debate
About?* says, at the bottom of page 3, that without the hockey
stick graph the 2001 IPCC report:

> would have been a very different document, it would not
> have been able to conclude what it did, nor could the
> IPCC have convinced world leaders to take the actions
> they subsequently took.

See the paper here: WebCitation.org/**61zHysZHp**

32-8

The discussion about published papers being merely advertising appears on page 5 here: webcitation.org/**5r4Q8z4Ne**

32-9

Regarding Mann's visit to the University of Nebraska see:

- WebCitation.org/**609nNwPCj**
- WebCitation.org/**609nJAs15**

32-10

The Wegman Report says, on page 3, that an error in the first Mann hockey stick paper:

> may be easily overlooked by someone not trained in statistical methodology. We note that there is no evidence that Dr. Mann or any of the other authors in paleoclimatology studies have had significant interactions with mainstream statisticians...It is important to note the isolation of the paleoclimate community; even though they rely heavily on statistical methods they do not seem to be interacting with the statistical community.

The entire 91-page Wegman Report, dated 2006, is available at: WebCitation.org/**6246QGvSt**

In May 2011, a paper derived from the Wegman Report was retracted by a scholarly journal due to the way it discussed tree rings. This problematic tree ring discussion also appeared in the introduction of the Wegman Report itself.

In the judgment of the journal editors the paper contained "portions of other authors' writings on the same topic in other publications, without sufficient attribution to these earlier works being given."

In other words, parts of the tree ring section of the Wegman Report were cut-and-pasted from elsewhere and proper credit was not given.

Those who would argue that Wegman's observations about climate scientists and statistics are invalidated by this controversy may wish to remember that I've identified 11 copy-and-paste examples in the 1995 IPCC health chapter (see Chapter 29 of this book, beginning on page 126). Nowhere does the IPCC acknowledge the original source of this material.

Should every other statement in the 1995 Climate Bible be rejected because one section contained cut-and-pasted material?

33-1

The discussion about the IPCC's peer-review process appears on pages 141-143 of the Boehmer-Christiansen and Kellow book titled *International Environmental Policy: Interests and the Failure of the Kyoto Process.*

Amazon.com claims this book was published in January 2003, but the book itself gives 2002 as the date.

33-2

See the InterAcademy Council report here:

http://reviewipcc.interacademycouncil.net/report.html

The PDF page number appears first, followed by those printed on the pages themselves in brackets:

- the Himalayan glacier discussion is on p. 40 (22)
- "significant improvements..." p. 43 (25)
- "truly independent..." p.39 (21)
- "recognized legitimacy and capacity..." p. 39 (21)

34-1

See the InterAcademy Council report here:

http://reviewipcc.interacademycouncil.net/report.html

The PDF page number appears first, followed by those printed on the pages themselves in brackets:

- "clear that these procedures are not always followed" p. 35 (17)
- "statements for which there is little evidence" pp. 17 and 57 (xv and 39)
- a "12-year appointment...is too long..." p. 64 (46)
- "significant shortcomings in each major step..." p. 31 (13)

34-2

See the InterAcademy Council report here:
http://reviewipcc.interacademycouncil.net/report.html
The PDF page number appears first, followed by those printed on the pages themselves in brackets:

- "rigorous conflict-of-interest policy..." pp. 71 and 78 (53 and 60)
- "pay special attention to issues of independence..." page 71 (53)

34-3

See this IPCC document dated May 2011: WebCitation.org/ **61uhDAGul**. Pages five and six are essentially blank. As of that date the IPCC still didn't know how it would implement a conflict-of-interest policy.

Absent any explicit description of how the IPCC intends to enforce its conflict-of-interest guidelines - interim or otherwise - we're entitled to be skeptical about the real world results.

34-4

See the InterAcademy Council report here:
http://reviewipcc.interacademycouncil.net/report.html
The PDF page number appears first, followed by those printed on the pages themselves in brackets:

- "from outside of the climate community..." page 63 (45)
- see also pages 15 and 78 (pages xiii and 60)

34-5

The IPCC resolution may be found at 2.3.3 on page 2 of this document: WebCitation.org/**61uhKwEMj** It lists the five *advisory* members the IPCC appointed to its new Executive Committee - the head of the IPCC's Secretariat, plus the four heads of the IPCC's Technical Support Units (more info on these units may be seen at the bottom of this page: **www.ipcc.ch/organization/organization_secretariat.shtml**)

The IAC committee itself felt it was appropriate for the head of the Secretariat to be part of the new Executive committee. It is the IPCC's substitution of its four staff members for three independent voices that is the problem.

These staff members are quintessential IPCC insiders - the exact opposite of the what was recommended by the IAC report.

35-1

In January 2010, IPCC vice-chair Jean-Pascal van Ypersele told the BBC: "I don't see how one mistake in a 3,000-page report can damage the credibility of the overall report". (See: WebCitation.org/**61uhSdqTR**)

IPCC insider Ottmar Edenhofer similarly declared in the German news magazine *Der Spiegel*: "We shouldn't question the credibility of an almost 3,000-page report because of one error". (See: WebCitation.org/**61uhbIXI4**)

Similarly, on page 86 of the mammoth collection of Inter-Academy Council questionnaire answers someone remarks:

> it is amazing that a 3,000-page report compiled under intense pressure by fallible human beings has been so nearly free of errors. The telephone directory of a major city is of comparable size and surely has far more errors. This topic is greatly overblown...

See also page 46 in which someone else declares that the small number of errors in IPCC reports is "extraordinary." Those questionnaire answers, in the form of 678-page PDF, are here:

http://reviewipcc.**interacademycouncil.net/Comments.pdf**

Additionally, computer science professor Steve Easter-brook began a blog post in February 2010 as follows:

> I guess headlines like "An error found in one paragraph of a 3000 page IPCC report; climate science unaffected" wouldn't sell many newspapers. And so instead, the papers spin out the story that a few mistakes undermine the whole IPCC process.

See it here: WebCitation.org/**61uhmeZhe**

35-2

See, for example, the letter-to-the-editor of the *Financial Times*, dated April 9, 2010 and signed by the President of the UK's Royal Society and the President of the US National Academy of Sciences. The leaders of these esteemed science bodies declare:

> as your editorial acknowledges, neither recent controversies, nor the recent cold weather, negate the consensus among scientists: something unprecedented is now happening.

36-1

See the PDF at **NOconsensus.org/AR5_authors.pdf.** As this book went to press Hilary Ostrov drew my attention to an updated list. I had no opportunity to examine it, but it may be seen here: WebCitation.org/**623sTasdY**

NEED MORE DETAIL?

The PDF edition of this book contains 1,400 embedded links that take you directly to the source material cited here. It may be purchased for $4.99 at:
TinyUrl.com/ipcc-expose

~

The following index includes proper names – people, organizations, institutions, and publications. Digital editions of this book permit you to search the entire book for any word of your choosing.

INDEX OF PROPER NAMES

CPSIA information can be obtained at www.ICGtesting.com
Printed in the USA
LVOW041539061211

258098LV00001B/23/P